My Promise is the Palace, so what am I doing in the Pit?

Riveting Answers to "Why Me, God?"

My Promise is the Palace, so what am I doing in the Pit?

Riveting Answers to "Why Me, God?"

by

ROD PARSLEY

Columbus, Ohio
U.S.A.

My Promise is the Palace, so what am I doing in the Pit?
Riveting Answers to "Why Me, God?"
Copyright © 1993 by Rod Parsley.
All rights reserved.
Printed in the United States of America.
ISBN 1-880244-14-4

Published by:
Results Publishing
World Harvest Church
P.O. Box 32932
Columbus, Ohio 43232
U.S.A.

Unless otherwise noted, all Scripture references are from the
King James Version of the Bible.

"Scripture taken from the HOLY BIBLE, NEW INTERNA-
TIONAL VERSION Copyright © 1973, 1978, 1984 Interna-
tional Bible Society. Used by permission of Zondervan Bible
Publishers."

TABLE OF CONTENTS

The Lord God hath given me the tongue of the learned, that I should know how to speak a word in season to him that is weary (Isaiah 50:4).

INTRODUCTION

"Why is my Life in the Pit?"

Pits are deep, dark sunken places ... definitely not designed for human habitation!

Joseph's brothers intended to kill him when they threw him down in an empty, man-made water pit in the wilderness (Genesis 37:22).

Pits are dangerous dungeons of darkness and death.

In biblical times, pits were frequently used as traps to ensnare an enemy or to catch an animal.

Pits were huge, seemingly inescapable holes in the ground ... the deepest, darkest parts of the earth ... uninhabitable, undesirable and, ultimately, unsurvivable.

Modern-Day Pits

Now the word *pit* is often used to describe a miserable situation that seems so hopeless there is no apparent

7

way out. Many Christians today believe they are at the bottom of a hopeless pit of trouble, without any ropes, any ladders or any friends to pull them out of their predicament. They feel trapped and alone, held hostage by their circumstances. With no apparent hope on the horizon, they accept defeat and give up.

So many of these Christians come to me in the midst of their despair with tearful testimonies of, "Pastor Rod, my life is in the pit. I have no way out. My finances are so bad I can't even afford to pay attention. My marriage relationship is so mangled that my wife breathes a silent prayer of thanksgiving when I leave for work. The only thing that eases my pain is when I pass out for a few hours in an alcoholic stupor."

These desperate pleas for help are real, and they demand real answers.

A Way Out

God has given me revelation from His Word for those in the pits ... principles which offer hope and healing to those wallowing in the depths of despair and hopelessness. Whether you are mired in the darkness of the pits right now or you know of someone who is floundering in his circumstances, this book will reveal God's Word and His plan for your life!

Pits Do Exist

Unquestionably, pits still exist!

Evidence is everywhere.

I've met too many single mothers who are mired in the depths of financial despair, unable to pay their next light bill or buy their next tank of gas ... let alone buy Christmas gifts or new school clothes for their children.

I know too many people snared in the addictive pit of drugs or alcohol. On the outside, these men and women seem normal enough; many lead seemingly productive lives. Yet inside they are lonely and isolated from their spouses and communities, tormented by demons they do not comprehend.

I've met too many men seduced by pornography and other sexual addictions ... without any apparent way out of the dungeon of their habitual seeking of short-lived pleasure. Their marriage relationships are dying, yet they seem incapable of stopping their sordid slide to the depths of depravity.

I know too many hard-working men wallowing in frustration and despair because it seems that no matter what they do, it is never enough to provide for their families. They feel emasculated and useless, with nothing on the horizon to lift them from their murky mess.

I've met too many widows sentenced to a lifetime of loneliness, living so deep in depression they seem incapable of climbing out of their social isolation. Thanksgiving, Christmas and all the other traditional times of family celebration represent moments of mourning rather than times of rejoicing.

I've talked with too many people whose marriages were tossed into the pit of absolute despair, devoid of any hope for new life for their dead relationships. I've seen too many troubled children carelessly tossed to and fro on the sorry scrap-heaps of those marriages.

I cannot deny it ... life has plenty of pits!

In the midst of their pit experiences, many Christians are crying out to God, "Lord, why are you picking on me? Why are you doing this to me and my family? What have I done wrong? Lord, if my promise is the palace, then what in the world am I doing in the pit?"

These are riveting questions that plague the minds of every born-again believer. But God's Word resolves these plaguing questions. When the skies are not blue, when the air is not sweet, when we are in the tomb and it is sealed, when we are suffocating from the stench of our own human experience ... we will come to know what it all means.

Some say, "I never have a bad day or the kind of problems you are talking about."

I believe is it time for us to begin to look realistically at our lives.

You began having bad days the first moment the doctor slapped you on the bottom, and you have been having bad days ever since. You are going to continue to have bad days, so just grab yourself by your spiritual boot straps and jerk yourself up. God has a plan for you!

Yes, there are times when you dance around the altar in absolute joy. But no one knows about the times when you go home at night, put your face down in a pillow to keep your family from hearing ... and you weep tears that well up from the depths of your hurting soul.

God knows about those times.

Call unto me, and I will answer thee, and shew thee great and mighty things, which thou knowest not (Jeremiah 33:3).

We serve a sovereign God, and He is in control.

You are His and He is yours.

He did not pay half-price for you.

God paid FULL PRICE, and He has a plan and a purpose for your life!

The A to Z of God's Plan

God has a future for you, and you can find it.

He is our Alpha and Omega. He is the beginning and the end. He shows us where we are, and He shows us where we are going to end up.

He shows us A and Z, but He doesn't always show us L, M, N, O, P or Q, R, S, T. If you are going to make

11

it all the way from the promise to the palace, you will have to pass through the P's.

Problems.

Persecutions.

People.

Then you must move through the T's.

Trials.

Tribulations.

Temptations.

You'll have to go through them on your way to the palace.

God, in His foreknowledge, did not just casually declare that you are going to end up at a certain place.

He has a master plan; He made a blueprint!

He knows just what it is going to take to get you from where you are to where He said you would be!

Where is God in your Trials?

I once heard a fellow describe his version of God, saying, "He's sitting up in the heavens with His feet hanging off a cloud and a huge pile of darts by His side. He delights in tossing these darts down at me and watching me scream in pain every time they hit my finances, or my marriage or some other area of my life."

This man was in the pit.

He did not understand God, and he did not understand

the plan God had for his life. You too may be crying, "Why me?" because you feel as if God is throwing darts at you.

The answer is in the Bible, and the answer will eliminate this and similar questions ... for the rest of your life!

If you are in the pit, I have good news for you ... you don't have to stay bogged down in the muck of life forever!

Like Joseph, you may be in a pit and convinced there is no way out.

And they took him, and cast him into a pit: and the pit was empty, there was no water in it (Genesis 37:24).

But there was a way out for Joseph, and there is a way out for you!

Joseph was delivered from his pit, and brought to Egypt where he ended up in Potiphar's house -- the captain of the guards.

In his youth Joseph received a vision from God that essentially said, "Here's where you are right now, Joseph, but over there is where you're going to end up. You're going to end up in the palace. Your brothers are going to bow down in worship to you. Now come on, Joseph, let's go. We're leaving point A and we're on our way to the palace!" (Genesis 37:10).

Between A and Z, Joseph had many detours, many problems and many perils. After he was rescued from the pit, he was established in Potiphar's house, where his master's wife tried to seduce him (Genesis 39:7). When he refused her advances, she falsely accused him of attempting to rape her.

Joseph's next stop was prison; but God watched over Joseph, even in prison.

But the Lord was with Joseph, and shewed him mercy, and gave him favour in the sight of the keeper of the prison (Genesis 39:21).

Joseph never lost heart, and ultimately, God gave him a time when he could interpret the Pharaoh's dreams. This brought Joseph out of prison and into the palace!

And Pharaoh said unto Joseph, Forasmuch as God hath shewed thee all this, there is none so discreet and wise as thou art:

Thou shalt be over my house, and according unto thy word shall all my people be ruled: only in the throne will I be greater than thou (Genesis 41:39,40).

A Purpose for the Pit

There was a reason why Joseph was in the pit.

There was a reason for his stay in Potiphar's house.

And, there is a reason for your own pit experience.

The problem is that most Christians do not have any idea what that purpose is! As you read these pages you will come to better understand God's special plan for you.

God has a word for those who are weary, distraught and disconnected.

God has a word for those who are oppressed, depressed and obsessed.

God has a word, and His word is always right on time!

The Lord God hath given me the tongue of the learned, that I should know how to speak a word in season to him that is weary (Isaiah 50:4).

Notice who gives.

It is not the radio or TV preacher, mama or daddy, grandma or grandpa ... but the Lord!

In eternity past, Jesus was given a word for eternity future by the Father.

Think about it.

Before your daddy ever knew your mama, before your granddaddy ever knew your grandmama, before your great grandparents ever knew one another, God knew you!

He saw you.

He was acquainted with you!

He knew your successes and was acquainted with your downfalls. He knew where you would be, when you would be there, and how you would get there. God, in His omniscient wisdom, looked out into eternity future and said, "This is where you are going to be at this time in your life -- walking through what you have to walk through -- so I can get you where I said you'd go!"

Many of you are just about to give up, to quit.

You have prayed until you can't pray anymore.

You have talked until you can't talk at all. Rhetoric and dialogue have lost their power, and you have exhausted all your human resources. Your religion no longer has the answers. A new theology hasn't helped. You have experimented with every doctrine known to man, and you have come to the end of human power.

It is time you realized He is Jehovah Shammah -- our God who is always there -- and He is standing next to you. He knew you would be in the pit, and He has already spoken a word for you. Today, that word is in season!

Jesus is saying, "There's an area in your life that is dead right now, but don't worry about it. I won't be late; I will be right on time! I have a word for you that will resurrect you. You will invade your future with destiny and purpose!"

Death Stinks

I am crucified with Christ: nevertheless I live; yet not I, but Christ liveth in me: and the life which I now live in the flesh I live by the faith of the Son of God, who loved me, and gave himself for me (Galatians 2:20).

Like Christ, you too must experience death.

There is a paradox.

You are a living dead person, and dead men don't do anything but stink. When Jesus' body was in that tomb,

Mary and the other Mary woke up early in the morning and went to the sepulchre to anoint His body.

Why?

Because it was dead and starting to stink. The Son of God was dead, so the two Marys came to the sepulchre to anoint his body. When the anointing comes, the stench of human flesh is erased.

The anointing is the supernatural enabling of God to empower you to speak words of life when your flesh is being crucified. It will enable you to see the resurrection when you are on the cross, and to speak words of deliverance when you are in prison.

It will cause you to prosper when you do not have a dollar to change. The anointing will give you joy when sorrow surrounds you, and victory in the midst of apparent defeat!

There is a supernatural enduing of power by God, through the Holy Ghost, that will keep your flesh from stinking when it should stink. There is a supernatural enabling from God that will take you from the pit to the palace ... no matter what your circumstances are today.

Goodbye Pitfalls

Even when you climb out of the pit, there are still plenty of pitfalls to dodge. Life is full of pitfalls!

We live in the throes of perilous times; men's hearts fail them for fear. We do not know how to avoid the pitfalls of life. Children and criminals alike roam our city streets armed with automatic weapons. America is running wild because God has been taken from the schools, out of the songbooks and from the church.

But on the darkest day, in the midst of these pitfalls, the light of God shines the brightest.

I have seen these pitfalls and perilous times through the eyes of an eternal God, and His plan for us declares there is nothing wrong in America that what is right in America cannot change!

His plan for your life declares there is nothing wrong in your body that what is right in His body cannot heal!

His provision boldly announces that there is nothing wrong in your house that what is right in His house cannot fix. There is no need in your life for which He has not already provided!

God knows who you are and He has a predestined, divine assignment for your life. His desire is to take you out of the pit and put you into the palace!

Jesus Stopped Satan

I believe is was Dr. Oral Roberts who said, "Jesus came to take off what the devil put on you and to put back on you everything the devil took off." Jesus came to stop the forces of hell that are ravaging and raping your life!

Jesus came to put up a "NO ENTRY" sign around

your soul, written in His blood. That supernatural sign stops the devil cold. Jesus sits in resurrected splendor, pointing His finger under the nose of the devil, declaring, "I am Alpha and I am Omega! I am He that was dead, but I am alive forevermore and you cannot touch my beloved unless you come through Me" (Revelation 1:8).

Religiosity Belongs in the Pit

I believe the church is packing up religious traditionalism -- and every other kind of "ism" like paganism and modernism -- and casting them out. The church is looking for the cloud by day and the pillar of fire by night. The church is looking for God to move, and is packing up to move with Him.

When God says "Get up," the church is going to get up.

When God says "Go forward," the church is going to go forward.

We must reach the point of complete personal abandonment so when God says "change your lifestyle, move to another city, or even resign your church" you are going to dance as you do it!

When God says "Move out of that old, dead, cold pit," you are going to pack your bags and move on out.

When God says "Get out of the bed of affliction," you are going to rise up.

19

When the Lord gets ready to move the church out of the pit and into the palace, be prepared to move!

God is sounding the horn and rallying His people as He prepares to pour out His Spirit in a mighty demonstration of His power in these last days.

And it shall come to pass afterward, that I will pour out my spirit upon all flesh; and your sons and your daughters shall prophesy, your old men shall dream dreams, and your young men shall see visions (Joel 2:28).

You and I are part of the triumphant, blood-bought, Holy Ghost filled, church of Jesus Christ against which the very gates of hell cannot prevail (Matthew 16:18)!

Do not fear those gates!

They cannot hold back the predestined plan of God.

The gates of hell CANNOT withstand the church when it moves in the power and demonstration of the Holy Ghost!

It is time to climb out of the pit of defeat, discouragement, failure, fear, addiction, bondage and poverty!

It is time to say to the devil, "You're not keeping me in any pit! No, not me! I have my eyes on the palace!"

God has given us not only natural eyes but spirit eyes, not only natural ears but spirit ears, not only natural hands but spirit hands. In the spirit, we can see what cannot be seen, and know what cannot be known and accomplish what cannot be accomplished!

While we look not at things which are seen, but at the things which are not seen: for the things which are seen are temporal (2 Corinthians 4:18).

This passage might be better translated, "The things which are seen are subject to change." Our natural man resists change and wants to stay in a comfortable, familiar world ... even if that world is a pit. But remember this: the author of the status quo is not Jehovah; his name is Satan!

Are you ready to change?

Are you ready to abandon the pit for the palace?

Are you ready to destroy the status quo in your life?

Once you grasp God's vision for your life you will no longer be satisfied with church as usual. You won't be satisfied with a six-foot icicle standing behind the pulpit spouting his three points and a poem. You will cry, "Where are the signs and wonders? Where are the miracles? Where is the revelation and the demonstration?

If America is ever going to be saved, it will be through a blood-bought, remnant church against which the gates of hell cannot prevail ... a church flowing in the message of the cross and the miracle of the resurrection!

Ignore Your Current Circumstances

Wherever you are -- pit, path or palace -- you have been preordained to climb to the glory and blessing of

Almighty God!

God has a plan for your life. He sent His anointing to impact your family, your church, your city and your nation with the Gospel of Jesus Christ.

I believe once you grasp His vision and submit to His plan and purpose, the gifts of the Spirit are going to begin to operate through you in power and demonstration.

I believe we are standing on the precipice of the greatest outpouring of the Spirit of God the world has ever known.

I believe you are destined to rise to a new dimension -- a higher height and deeper depth in the things of God. A revelation of His purpose and plan for the church is going to be birthed in you, and YOU are going to...

Take up serpents; and if they drink any deadly thing, it shall not hurt them; they shall lay hands on the sick, and they shall recover (Mark 16:18).

CHAPTER ONE
"You Mean there's a Purpose to the Pit?"

The universe is not just whirling madly in a darkened abyss of meaningless nothing.

There is reason, purpose, and design to the world you live in.

If the sun was closer to the earth, our planet would be a charred cinder.

If the sun was farther away from the earth, we would be entombed in a gigantic deep freeze, so cold no life could exist.

But God is a God of purpose.

The sun sits precisely where it sits in God's universe because that is the way He designed it!

You see with your eyes, not with your nose because He's a God of purpose. You hear with your ears, not with your feet, because God's plan for your ears was different than His plan for your feet!

He is a God of design.

In your body there is a complicated highway system of veins and arteries sufficient to carry life-giving blood to every cell.

Our God is a God of order.

We are not serving a God who has us running around,

like a mouse in a maze, saying, "Whoops, that must not have been God. I had better go in this direction." You go a little further and run headlong again into a closed door, bounce back and say, "Well, that must not be the will of God." Finally, you turn a corner and find an open door, so you think you have to go through it.

You are not a mouse, and our God is not a maze maker. Stop trying doors. Walk in the will of God. Then if you come to a closed door God said to go through, kick it down, in the name of Jesus.

Don't be led captive by an angel of light standing behind an open door beckoning you to come. Walking in the will of God brings spiritual discernment to see things as they really are.

Our Father has a plan!

But remember, we do not always see the L, M, N, O, P of His plan. Often we only see A and Z. We are serving a God who is capable and willing to successfully navigate our lives from where we are to where He said we are going to end up.

The Bible says the steps of a good man are ordered by the Lord (Psalm 37:23). You pick your feet up, and He puts them down.

You are the seed that could. When your father and mother conceived you, there were tens of thousands of other seeds on a race through your mother's fallopian tubes. And you are the one that made it.

He has a plan and purpose for your life.

God, in the eternal past, looked down through the corridor of time and space. He knew where your parents would have to be and what they would have to do to have you at precisely the right place at precisely the right time.

God knew how steel would be made and where ceiling tiles would be manufactured. He brought someone to the knowledge of how to pour concrete so there would be a foundation for your church building.

Why? He would then have you in position to receive His message and direction that you need for your life.

Always remember, you do not find the will of God ... you are in it! You are walking in the perfect will of Almighty God right now.

But you say, "Pastor Rod, L, M, N, O, P - what about those P words ... problems, pits, and persecution? What about those T words ... trouble, trial, and temptation?"

God knows all about your troubles, trials, and temptations. If you have them, He has allowed them. They serve a purpose; and, like Joseph, He will give you the strength to walk through them. Stop shaking your fist at God and crying, "Lord, why are you allowing me to wallow in the pit?"

I want you to have a revelation of the God you serve that will forever eclipse your cries of, "Why me?" and

"Woe is me," and "Why is everybody always picking on me?"

Trial into Triumph!

I don't believe anyone who stands in a pulpit and tells you that you will never have to go through the P's and the T's on your way to Z. To say you will never go through the P's and the T's is an injustice to the plan and purpose God desires to work in your life.

Some of the trials and tribulations you are going through are the design, the plan and the purpose of God.

A sweet lady came up to me after church not long ago and said, "Pastor Rod, I'm going through this and I'm going through that." Before she could get through telling me, I just started dancing.

She said, "Don't you understand what I'm going through? How can you dance when I just told you all the trials and tribulations in my life?"

I said, "Listen to the confession of your own mouth. You just told me you're going through. That means whatever trial you are in, you aren't staying. You're coming out on the other side with your hands lifted up, shouting the praises of the God that not only brought you out, but put you in and took you through."

Learn to love the trial, the tribulation and the temptation. Why?

Because in every pit, in every trial, in every tribulation, in every temptation, He has a reason for it ... and He has planned your escape!

Your problems will be eclipsed by His power; your trials will become testimonies; your tribulations will turn to triumphs; your pit will be exchanged for a palace!

God has a purpose, a specific plan, for your life! If it were not so, at the moment you prayed, "Heavenly Father, I'm a sinner and I need your grace. Wash me in your blood and give me eternal life" ... God would have catapulted you into His glorious presence. God saved you from eternity in hell, but He left you here for a reason. He does not do anything by accident.

Your life is proof of His purpose. Don't ever say again, "I was born on the wrong side of the tracks," or "I didn't have the educational opportunities others have had," or "I was born with the wrong color of skin."

The Spirit, not the Law

Therefore seeing we have this ministry, as we have received mercy, we faint not;

But have renounced the hidden things of dishonesty, not walking in craftiness, nor handling the word of God deceitfully; but by manifestation of the truth commending ourselves to every man's conscience in the sight of God (2 Corinthians 4:1,2).

God has a plan for you; He has a ministry and a specific purpose for your life! He has a design for your future, and you can rest in knowing He is going to give you the power to fullfill His plan!

Who also hath made us able ministers of the new testament; not of the letter, but of the spirit: for the letter killeth, but the spirit giveth life (2 Corinthians 3:6).

We have all been given a ministry, but your ministry is not to be governed by the flesh, where the pits are, but by the Spirit.

The letter kills. The letter shoves you in the pit, but the Spirit gives you the power and the life to reside in the palace! The Old Testament letter of the law set out hundreds of rules.

The Jews were in bondage to the law as they religiously tried to keep them. It was an impossible task.

We are troubled on every side, yet not distressed; we are perplexed, but not in despair; persecuted, but not forsaken; cast down, but not destroyed ... knowing that he which raised up the Lord Jesus shall raise up us also by Jesus (2 Corinthians 4:8,9,14).

Paul established that you have a ministry, by the mercy of God, if you faint not. Just like Paul, you will have trouble – you will find yourself in the pit. You'll have trouble on the right hand and on the left. There will be trouble in front of you, behind you and beneath you.

But you do not have to be distressed.

You may be perplexed, but you do not need to despair!

You may be persecuted, but you are not forsaken!

You may be cast down, but you are not destroyed.

When the devil comes against you with his most deadening blow to try to thwart the plan and purpose of God -- just like those toy Weebles -- you may wobble, but you won't fall down!

Unreasonable Peace in the Pit

You must learn to walk in God's peace, trusting in Him.

When you are troubled on every side, distressed, perplexed, cast down ... rest in the peace of God that is not produced by mental reasoning. Walking through the fiery trial, God says, "You are my child. I will not allow the crackling flames to kindle upon you."

This kind of peace is produced only by a supernatural knowledge, a revelation of God on a different level than perhaps you have ever known Him before. This kind of peace keeps you from wanting God to kill the king when He tells you to go into the fiery furnace. Instead, you will stand at the furnace door and say, "Heat it up seven times hotter if you want to, for the God I serve is able to deliver me. And whether He does or not, He is still God."

Knowing that he which raised up the Lord Jesus shall raise up us also by Jesus, and shall present us with you.

For all things are for your sakes, that the abundant grace might through the thanksgiving of many redound to the glory of God (2 Corinthians 4:14,15).

Paul knew something.

Shipwreck.

Snakebite.

Beaten with rods.

Left for dead.

All things are for your good!

For which cause we faint not; but though our outward man perish, yet our inward man is renewed day by day (2 Corinthians 4:16).

He renews us every morning, even when we're in the pit! (Lamentations 3:23)

And I saw heaven opened, and behold a white horse; and he that sat upon him was called Faithful and True (Revelation 19:11).

No matter how deep your pit is, you have a promise from God that He will remain faithful and true to His Word. You will be nourished and renewed day by day!

The Bible says your spirit shall help all of your infirmities (Proverbs 18:14). Feed your spirit, and you won't have to be concerned about what to eat, or wear, or where you will live. He knows your needs, and He will make provision for His servant on the divine journey to the palace.

But seek ye first the kingdom of God, and his righteousness; and all these things shall be added unto you. Take therefore no thought for the morrow (Matthew 6:33,34).

Paul was beaten with rods; He was left for dead. He was jailed, placed under house arrest.

What does he call it?

For our light affliction, which is but for a moment, worketh for us a far more exceeding and eternal weight of glory (2 Corinthians 4:17).

Paul calls his trials a "light affliction." Why?

Paul knew something!

He called his affliction just a momentary stop on the way to glory! How can Paul have such an attitude?

While we look not at the things which are seen, but at the things which are not seen: for the things which are seen are temporal (the actual translation is *subject to change); but the things which are not seen are eternal (2 Corinthians 4:18).*

Paul was trying to pull us up to this revelation of who our Heavenly Father really is. He was saying, "Hey, I know there are these little pesky problems that enter my life, but I don't pay attention to them. Instead, I focus on the things which are eternal, the things which will eventually bring me to glory with God."

31

Which Bread do You Eat?

Jesus confused His disciples when he announced to them,

For the bread of God is he which cometh down from heaven, and giveth life unto the world (John 6:33).

They responded, not understanding His meaning, *Lord ... give us this bread (v.34).*

He then told them,

I am the bread of life: he that cometh to me shall never hunger; and he that believeth on me shall never thirst (v.35).

Jesus then chastised His followers. To paraphrase His words, Jesus told them, "You're not following me because of the miraculous signs and wonders I've done. You're not following me because you see something that others can't see. You're following me because I put natural bread in your belly."

There are too many Christians with full bellies and no real revelation of who God is. They have full bellies, and thus miss the revelation of God which only their hunger could produce. When the plan of God is for them to be hungry, they miss Him. When the process of God is the valley low as well as the mountain high, they want to give up on God.

Here's the revelation Jesus gave His disciples. He said, *Your fathers did eat manna in the wilderness, and are dead. I am the living bread which came down from heaven: if any man eat this bread, he shall live for ever (John 6:49,51).*

Jesus was trying to draw them into the supernatural realm. He said, "If you will identify with me in my suffering and in my death, then you will identify with me in my resurrection from the dead and walking in the newness of life."

Like those early followers of Jesus, we spend too much of our time splashing around in the flatlands of shallow spiritual experience instead of walking in the Spirit.

That the God of our Lord Jesus Christ, the Father of glory, may give you the spirit of wisdom and revelation in the knowledge of him (Ephesians 1:17).

You cannot reason your way into this knowledge that makes you live the way Paul lived. He was troubled on every side, but not forsaken. Paul had tasted supernatural bread. Divine knowledge gave him supernatural ability to endure beatings, shipwreck, and imprisonment and still be able to say, "I am more than a conqueror in these light afflictions."

He was not ignoring the fact of what he was going through. He was not acting as if the problem did not exist. He was not ignoring the reality of imprisonment when he said, *And hath raised us up together, and made us sit together in heavenly places in Christ Jesus (Ephesians 2:6).*

Paul was living on another level.

He knew something.

He understood what Jesus knew when He walked up to that woman in the temple who was bent over for fourteen years, and said, *Woman, thou art loosed from thine infirmity (Luke 13:12).*

You and I need to come up to that same level of spiritual enlightenment.

The eyes of your understanding being enlightened; that ye may know what is the hope of his calling, and what the riches of the glory of his inheritance in the saints, and what is the exceeding greatness of his power to us-ward who believe, according to the working of his mighty power,

Which he wrought in Christ, when he raised him from the dead, and set him at his own right hand in the heavenly places, far above all principality, and power, and might, and dominion, and every name that is named, not only in this world, but also in that which is to come: and hath put all things under his feet (Ephesians 1:18-22).

Job had a Divine Revelation

There were those in the Bible and there are those living today who have a supernatural revelation of Jesus that other Christians do not have. I believe if we all had that kind of revelation of who He is, we would live differently, talk differently, act differently, move differently, shout dif-

34

ferently, sing differently and pray differently.

Job had a revelation of God.

His wife came to him as he sat on the ash heap of wreck and ruin, scraping his flesh with a potsherd. His children weren't sick; they were dead and buried -- all of them.

Job not only had no food in his house, he had no house to put any food in!

He had nothing.

He sat on an ash heap where his great wealth, his home and his family once were. His flocks were gone. His herds were gone. In the midst of this pathetic scene, his wife said, *Dost thou still retain thine integrity? curse God, and die (Job 2:9).*

She was saying, "Job, you're going to die anyway, so why don't you go ahead and curse God and hasten the process?"

Job's answer became clear later in the book when he said,

For I know that my redeemer liveth, and that he shall stand at the latter day upon the earth (Job 19:25).

Job had no prophet, no priest, no preacher, no Sunday school, no denomination headquarters, no church service, no padded pews. Job had no spaghetti dinners or bingo parlors. He had no committee to send posies to the hospital when he was sick. He had no Christian television or radio.

He had nothing but a supernatural revelation!

And that revelation of God brought him off the ash heap. Because of Job's supernatural revelation of God and His refusal to curse God when he was in the pit, the Lord blessed the latter portion of Job's life more than the former.

So the Lord blessed the latter end of Job more than his beginning: for he had fourteen thousand sheep, and six thousand camels, and a thousand yoke of oxen, and a thousand she asses.

He had also seven sons and three daughters. And he called the name of the first, Jemima; and the name of the second, Kezia; and the name of the third, Kerenhappuch. And in all the land were no women found so fair as the daughters of Job: and their father gave them inheritance among their brethren.

After this lived Job an hundred and forty years, and saw his sons, and his sons' sons, even four generations. So Job died, being old and full of days (Job 42:12-17).

God gave Job 140 years of life -- AFTER his trial in the pit was over!

He gave Job DOUBLE the wealth he had previously possessed!

All his former relatives and associates returned to pay respect to him and to bring him gifts (Job 42:7-15). And, he lived to see his sons and grandsons to four generations

(Job 42:16)!

Job knew something supernaturally. And that revelation of his Redeemer gave him the supernatural enabling to make it from the promise, through the pit, and to the palace.

I know, dear reader, it will do the same for you.

The word which came to Jeremiah from the Lord, saying, Arise, and go down to the potter's house, and there I will cause thee to hear my words.

Then I went down to the potter's house, and, behold, he wrought a work on the wheels (Jeremiah 18:1-3).

CHAPTER TWO

Lessons at the Potter's House

When my little girl, Ashton Blaire, was three-years-old, she was sitting on the bathroom counter one Sunday morning while I was getting ready for church. I pointed to her in the mirror and said, "Who is that?"

She just gave me a big grin in the mirror.

Then I said, "That's daddy's girl. That's Ashton."

She looked back at me as only a three-year-old can and, grabbing her nose, giggled, "Daddy, that's not Ashton. This is Ashton."

Although you reflect a mirrored image of God, you are not Him. That mirror image can't walk. It can't talk.

It can't eat or live. It doesn't have any life of its own, but that of the light reflected in it.

It is God which worketh in you both to will and to do of His good pleasure (Philippians 2:13).

You are the mirror reflecting the image of God, and without Him you do not live.

Jesus said, *I am the light of the world (John 8:12).*

Unless He shines on you, you cannot shine. Unless He breathes on you, you cannot breathe. Unless He walks in you, you cannot walk.

I am crucified with Christ: nevertheless I live; yet not I, but Christ liveth in me: and the life which I now live in the flesh I live by the faith of the Son of God, who loved me, and gave himself for me (Galatians 2:20).

We Serve a Sovereign God

He is God and you are not. There are many today who try to convince you that you are God ... but when was the last time you walked across the water in your swimming pool, displaying your omnipotence?

When was the last time you displayed your omniscience? When was the last time you knew where your kids were every second of the day?

When was the last time you displayed your omnipresence by being in church Sunday morning and down at the mall at the same time?

It takes only a few steps down the corridor of life to discover that we are just human. It takes little thought to realize that He is God and we are not.

Our purpose on this planet is to reflect who He is in everything we do.

God declared to Job,

Then the Lord answered Job out of the whirlwind, and said, Who is this that darkeneth counsel by words without knowledge? Gird up now thy loins like a man; for I will demand of thee, and answer thou me. (Job 38:1-3)

God is saying someone doesn't have any idea what he is talking about. Then He poses this piercing question to Job and to all mankind:

Where wast thou when I laid the foundations of the earth? declare, if thou hast understanding. Who hath laid the measures thereof, if thou knowest? or who hath stretched the line upon it? Whereupon are the foundations thereof fastened? or who laid the corner stone thereof;

When the morning stars sang together, and all the sons of God shouted for joy? Or who shut up the sea with doors, when it brake forth, as if it had issued out of the womb? (Job 38:4-8).

He is asking us, "Have you lived long enough to find out what the earth is and who laid the cornerstone? Do you know where light comes from and why the oceans, although upside down, don't spill from their boundaries?

You've lived a long time; answer me if you know."

The Apostle Paul spoke of the purpose and design of everything God has released into your life.

Therefore seeing we have this ministry, as we have received mercy, we faint not (2 Corinthians 4:1).

The word *ministry* is the Greek word *diaconia*. It means we are servants. Paul is saying we have been called into service -- and he's not talking about a church service. He's talking about your ministry -- your gift of service, whatever it may be, in the body of Christ.

We have all been called into service, but we are unable to fulfill that service unless we receive God's mercy. Mercy becomes the fuel on the fire that makes it possible for us to fulfill what God has called us to do.

You have been called for a purpose.

Paul said, *Walk worthy of the vocation wherewith ye are called (Ephesians 4:1).*

God has a job for you to do.

Not only does He have a plan for you, but He also has a purpose. His purpose requires His power, so He has made a plan to bring it to pass.

He is a sovereign God, and you have been predestined for a purpose. Without God, you do not have the power to fulfill the purpose of God for your life.

God's plan for you is much more than sitting in the church pew every Sunday morning until you go home to be with Him. He has a destiny for you to fulfill.

A Trip to the Potter's House

Let us journey with Jeremiah down to the Potter's house, and meet the Potter. There you will discover His plan and His purpose. There you will come to understand the purpose of your trials and tribulations and receive the answer to your wails of, "Why me, God?"

We peer through the dusty window of the Potter's house, and we see the Potter, the wheels and the clay.

We see a Creator of incredible ability and intent. We see an intelligent and capable craftsman. We see the tools the Potter uses to work His design, His will and His purpose in the clay.

We see the raw material of the clay, through which the intent and purpose of the Potter will be manifested.

He is the Potter, and we are that shapeless, purposeless clay.

We begin to study the Potter as he sits at the wheel, and we are amazed at the interest the Potter takes in the formless clay. As the wheel turns, He begins to apply pressure to the clay. His hands are massive and attest to incredible power and strength. But then we realize with what uncanny gentleness those hands begin to apply the pressure.

And now we see the Potter dipping His hands in water to make the clay pliable. And as He fashions the clay, His interest in the transformation He is working, by the pressure of His hands, is remarkable. Never is the gaze of His eyes distracted from His purpose as He molds the clay.

Do not be discouraged.

You are His workmanship, and He never lifts His eye from you. He sees you when you are shapeless.

He sees you when you are broken bread and poured out wine.

He sees you in the valley!

He sees you in the fire!

He sees you in the pit!

His eyes never lift from the work of His hands! You are not alone. Bask in the radiance of the gaze of the Almighty Creator as He fashions the work of your life upon His wheels.

The Wheels of Circumstance

In the wheels we find the circumstances the Potter uses to work His purpose in the clay. The wheel of the Potter is the trial, the problem, the pitfall, the circumstance that besets you today, the sum total of everything that is going on in your life.

The wheels are the tools of the Potter that brings His purpose to pass.

There will come a time when only the Potter and the clay remain. There will come a time when the wheels are incidental. They are necessary now, but they are only transitory instruments in the Potter's plan.

There is going to come a time when the trials, the tribulations, the tests, the temptations, Potiphar's house, the prison and the pit all fade into insignificance.

They will all be set aside. They are necessary right now for the Potter to perform His work in you, but there will come a time when He will set those wheels to the side. Like Joseph, you are not meant to perish in the pit you have tumbled headlong into.

What you are going through, you are just going through. God is working His plan in your life. Realize the loving attention of your Father as He works.

He dips His hands in the water of the Holy Ghost. He dips them in the Word of God as He fashions you on the wheel of life. At times you spin, losing all sense of direction. You don't know where you are going. You can't see the Potter, and you feel as if your life has been tossed in the air.

But just hold on, because very soon the wheel is going to stop turning, the pit will be behind you and the palace will be on the horizon. You will be a vessel of honor -- a vessel in the image and likeness of Almighty God!

Circumstances bombard us; pitfalls are all around us. We don't understand, we can't focus and we feel as if we are losing our grip.

You are not going to fall off the table. You are not going to perish in the depths of your trial.

He has His eyes on you.

He has His hands on you.

He is pressuring you with loving hands dipped in Holy Ghost water.

He is holding all things together by the power of His Word (Hebrews 1:3).

He is molding you!

Dead People Don't Have a Will

The relationship between the clay and the Potter speaks of the relationship between you and God -- the finite and the infinite; the powerless and the all powerful; the unknowing and the all knowing; the incapable and the all capable.

The Potter has absolute power over the clay.

But we say, "Now wait a minute, Pastor. The clay has no will, but I am full of will."

What, after all, is our "will?"

Will is the ability to make choices within a defined boundary.

The will you have been given tells of the sovereignty of the Potter over the clay -- of God over you. God created you with a will.

That *will* you are always carrying on about came from

God, and without Him you wouldn't even have it. He gave you the will to choose who would be your sovereign master.

The purpose of your will is to allow you to choose who you will serve -- God or the devil. He will never force Himself on you; the choice is yours.

Will is given to you by God, so don't toot your horn about your will. God gave you a will for the sole purpose of allowing you to choose who you would submit to.

The relationship between the clay and the Potter reflects our relationship with God.

We are pliable.

We are moldable.

We respond to the imprint of His hand.

The Potter does not put steel or lead on His wheel. He uses clay made pliable by His Word.

We are moldable in the hands of the Master.

We learn a lesson at the Potter's house. We learn that God is sovereign and has absolute authority over the clay.

We shrink from the sovereignty of the Potter, and justifiably so, because it means relinquishing control of our lives.

We are afraid to relinquish our lives into the sovereign care of God. Fear is the reason we are always trying to take back control of our lives.

We are unsure. After all, we cannot see Him.

Don't Jump

Then we realize there is purpose in the Potter's work. The Potter has a purpose in the pits and problems He uses to work the clay. But the purpose is known only to the Potter; it cannot be known by the clay.

We're at point A and we're going to point Z, but we want to know L, M, N, O, P. We want to know every step of the path to the palace, what's going to happen on the path and how God's going to get us to the palace.

God doesn't work that way. Why? He expects the submission and trust of the clay.

We cannot know the purpose any more than the clay can know the purpose of the Potter while it sits on the wheel. The only way the clay will ever know the purpose of the Potter is to be still.

Sit still. Don't jump off the wheel and run to the mirror to see how you look. Just sit there.

Be still and you shall see the salvation of the Lord in humble, quiet submission to the loving hands of the Potter. You will eventually see your purpose!

Sit still! Half the time we work ourselves right out of the will of God through spiritual calisthenics.

Be still, and know that I am God (Psalm 46:10).

"What are you going to use?" you say.

"I'm going to use those wheels, those pits, those problems and those circumstances."

The clay gains form and purpose from the Potter, but the Potter also gains from the clay. Without the clay, the Potter cannot bring His purpose to fruition. He cannot mold and make and give display to the beating of His heart.

Don't jump off! Stay on the wheel.

He Loves You

You may be in the pit, but He loves you enough to bring you to the palace.

You may be in Potiphar's house, but He loves you enough to bring you to the palace.

You may be in prison, but He loves you enough to bring you to the palace.

Without recognition of His love, we cannot submit to His sovereign rule in our lives. We are afraid of it. We don't know what He might do. Even when we know He has a purpose for us we still tremble, because we don't know what His purpose might be.

But we see Him in the garden and hear Him pray, *Not my will, but thine, be done (Luke 22:42).* We see Him beaten, and every drop of blood that falls cries out, "He's doing this for you." With every step He takes, the earth shouts, "He loves you."

We see Him carry that rugged beam.

Standing at the base of an old rugged cross, we see

His love. We see Him hang His head in sorrow and give up the ghost. With His final breath His piercing eyes penetrate my calloused heart and tell me that no matter what I have done or where I am, the Potter loves the clay. My mind resounds with the declaration, *Greater love hath no man than this, that a man would lay down his life for his friends (John 15:13).*

He did not lay down His life because He had to. He said, *No man taketh it from me, but I lay it down of myself. I have power to lay it down, and I have power to take it again (John 10:18).*

He said, "I'll show you how much I love you. You deserve to go to hell, but so you don't have to go, I'll go for you."

He defeated the devil that had defeated you and, in resurrection power, said, *because I live, you can live also (John 14:19).*

He died for you.

Who Is He?

God is not just Jehovah Shammah, our ever present help ... Jehovah Shalom, our God of perfect peace ... Jehovah Tsidkenu, our God of righteousness ... Jehovah M'Kaddesh, our holiness ... Jehovah Rophe, our healer ... Jehovah Nissi, our banner of completed victory ... Jehovah Rohi, our Shepherd.

He is not just El Shaddai, our God who is all sufficient.

He is not just the King of Zion and Judah's lion.

He is much more.

If you put all of God's characteristics into a pot and boiled them down, they would boil down to one all-encompassing element of His divine nature: LOVE.

Because we know His love, we cannot only endure our times in the pit but we can rejoice in them.

Not only must we have a revelation of His absolute authority over our lives, but we must also have a revelation of who He is.

God is love.

You will never make it from the pit, prison, Potiphar's house, and through the wilderness if you do not know His love for you.

If you understand that God is love and God is sovereign, then no matter what you are going through, you will know He is using that circumstance to work His purpose in your life.

We become off balance on the potter's wheel. He has us in the pits of our circumstances. Sometimes we can't even see Him. Sometimes we can only catch a glimpse of Him as we are whirled along on the path to the palace.

We want to climb down from the wheel.

But we hold on because we would rather feel the

touch of the Master's hands. We would rather feel the pressure of what He is taking us through than live a life without Him. We yield our lives to the Potter because we trust Him.

We are willing to stay on the wheel because we know He is working His purpose.

It may look like He has kicked us out of the nest, it may feel like we are falling and about to smash on the rocks of wreck and ruin. But just before we shatter, His everlasting arms reach out and break our fall.

It doesn't matter what He takes you through.

It doesn't matter!

He loves you. Though you go through the fire, you will not smell of smoke. He will command the crackling flames not to kindle upon you (Daniel 3:27).

You Cannot do It on Your Own

You are the clay. He is the Potter. You are the vessel He has chosen to use to fulfill His purpose in the earth. Just as the clay is unable to do anything of itself, so are you unable to fulfill the purpose of God through your own efforts.

God's purpose for your life is not just to read the Bible. It is not just to pray. It is not just to go to church.

God requires all those things, but they are not His purpose for your life.

He has a plan He wants to work on this earth through you, and all those other things are just part of your relationship with Him.

Everyone thinks, "Well, I'm serving God. I'm doing what God called me to do because I go to church."

No, you go to church to celebrate Him. You go to church to praise Him for the power He has given you to perform the purpose He has destined for your life.

Earthen Vessels

But we have this treasure in earthen vessels, that the excellency of the power may be of God, and not of us (2 Corinthians 4:7).

Paul is writing about clay pots made from the dust of the ground -- not gold or silver vessels.

He is writing about vessels made from the clay the Potter puts on His wheel and shapes and fashions after His own good pleasure. What was useless and purposeless clay becomes a thing of beauty, utility and purposefulness.

And the Lord God formed man of the dust of the ground, and breathed into his nostrils the breath of life; and man became a living soul (Genesis 2:7).

You are a clay pot.

God is going to bring you to the point in your life where you can't do it on your own. He is going to take you from pit to trial to tribulation until you cry out, "I must have you or I will die!"

What is the purpose of a vessel? To be filled!

A vessel is created empty -- empty of its will, empty of its desires, empty of its plans, empty of its destiny.

Why? It's dead.

It's a dead vessel.

Then I went down to the potter's house, and, behold, he wrought a work on the wheels. And the vessel that he made of clay was marred in the hand of the potter: so he made it again another vessel, as seemed good to the potter to make it (Jeremiah 18:3,4).

The clay cannot know the purpose. Only the Potter knows the purpose. The clay only finds its purpose in absolute total submission -- even unto death.

Jesus was resurrected through submission to the Father. The purpose of God was resurrection, but the plan of God to accomplish that purpose was crucifixion.

The frailty of our human flesh becomes caught between the wheels of plan and purpose. But if the clay will hold on through crucifixion, it will come to resurrection.

Don't quit in the middle of the plan.

Hold on and you'll see the purpose for the pit you're in!

You may have been afraid to relinquish control of your life to the sovereign will of God, but you have seen the Potter.

You have seen His love.

He has a plan.

He has a purpose.

He has a plan He is ready to work in your life. He is only waiting for <u>you</u> to quit playing god in your life, so He can take control.

Begin now with the person of the loving Potter, our God of love. Submit to the principle that He is God and you are not. Submit to His sovereign control of your life.

You will find purpose and become the handiwork and workmanship of a loving God. You will find hope that tomorrow will be different than today.

He is ready to mold you and make you. He is waiting to take you from the pit to the palace.

Write the vision, and make it plain upon tables, that he may run that readeth it. For the vision is yet for an appointed time, but at the end it shall speak, and not lie: though it tarry, wait for it; because it will surely come, it will not tarry (Habakkuk 2:2,3).

CHAPTER THREE

The Road Map to the Palace

The prophetic vision is God's road map that shows us the way to the palace. His prophetic vision also guides the church along the path to the palace.

His vision will empower the church of Jesus Christ to take the Word straight into the pit and say, "Here is the answer. Here is your escape. Here is your road map to the palace."

The Greek word for church is *ecclesia* meaning *the called out ones*. In the New Testament, the *ecclesia* refers to a body of free citizens called together by a herald.

Today, the Holy Ghost calls. Some answer, some do not.

If you want to be one of the "called out ones", then you must understand what God is doing with you when you are in the pit. You must be hungry with desire, and you must be willing to receive a vision -- a revelation -- of how God intends to take you to the palace.

The Vision of the Palace

The vision of God's ultimate will for your life (the vision of the palace) is given through His visionaries.

In the local church, God gives that road map to the palace through a visionary -- not a group, a single visionary. In the local church that visionary is <u>always</u> the pastor.

In His plan and purpose, God calls specific men and women, gives them a vision, and then surrounds them with the people to bring that vision to pass.

As a pastor, it is my responsibility to seek God's path to the palace for my congregation, and then give them a detailed spiritual road map on how to make that journey. To seek that path, at the end of every year I shut myself in with God to receive specific, prophetic direction for my church for the next year. Every year His words have built upon the previous year's direction.

The Road is Created ... Stone by Stone

God never gives you the entire vision all at once. If He did, we would be so overwhelmed we would turn and run as fast as our feet could carry us.

He reveals His plan and purpose in stages. The path to the palace is one we follow stone by stone. His vision is for an appointed time; and as the time comes, another stepping stone is revealed.

The path to the palace is for the entire body of Christ. The body of Christ is anxious to crawl out of the pit and discern the path to the palace, to see the plan and purpose of God in these final hours of the age.

Isaiah 58:12 laid the first stone on that path of revelation -- a rallying call to a sleeping church.

And they that shall be of thee shall build the old waste places: thou shalt raise up the foundations of many generations; and thou shalt be called, The repairer of the breach, The restorer of paths to dwell in.

The devil tried to steal the basic tenets of our faith. He tried to steal the born again experience and the baptism in the Holy Ghost. He tried to steal freedom and deliverance. He tried to steal healing and holiness. He tried to steal the hope that rests within us for the rapture of the church; the resurrection of the saints; the second coming of Jesus Christ; and the reality of an eternal heaven and hell.

But as the church roused from its lethargy in the pit of religiosity, it loudly declared, "We are the restorers of paths to dwell in." We served notice on the devil and began repaving the path to the palace.

That first revelation awakened many in the sleeping church.

They are no longer asleep, and I believe thousands of Christians are seeking the true Gospel. Men and women no longer flounder at the foot of the cross with no understanding of a resurrected Christ. They are leaving depravation and entering into the freedom and forgiveness of God.

The next revelation stone is found through studying what the Bible teaches about leaven. Leaven represents sin, and *a little leaven leaveneth the whole lump (Galatians 5:9)*. Only a pure and holy church, free of the leaven of a sinful world, will bring about revival.

Sin quietly crept into the church. God's Word to us in the New Testament clearly reveals the five forms of Satan's debilitating leaven that traps churches and Christians alike in pits of religiosity, presumption, worldliness, immorality and legalism.

In the progression of God's plan of provision for this group, we see the next stone. He has given us a road map to freedom and absolute victory -- in our own lives and in the church of Jesus Christ!

Endtime Revival

Every major movement of God has been born in the heat of revival, with miracles, signs, wonders and demonstration of the gifts of the Spirit.

But as soon as revival begins, man rushes to label it, and before you know it he is inviting everyone to come worship at the new shrine of religiosity. Then we again splash contentedly in the muddy water of yesterday's revival flood, singing, "It is beginning to rain."

There is no water in the pit, and it is not raining in the puddles!

It is time for the church to leave the pit. It's time to stop wading in the puddles and dive into the ocean of revelation. It's time to start depending on the supernatural for our survival!

God said, *But the land, whither ye go to possess it, is a land of hills and valleys, and drinketh water of the rain of heaven. (Deuteronomy 11:11)*

Once you bathe in that water, you cannot go back to the old stream. You have experienced too much cleansing to go back. You've had a drink of living water, a taste of living bread, and you cannot go back to pabulum.

Once you have the vision -- the road map -- RUN with it! Proclaim loudly, "Jesus is coming, Jesus is coming, and I know the way to His palace!"

Once the vision pulls you from the pit, no man or man made institution can ever hold you in that pit again. When you see the vision for the palace, you are not afraid of what the denomination thinks, or what the board thinks, or what your church members think, or what your wife thinks or, for that matter, what you think about the situation.

Why?

Because you have a road map, a clear vision, and in that vision there is protection. As long as you operate in the vision, God gives you the anointing to destroy every yoke!

The Palace Vision

And they that shall be of thee shall build the old waste places: thou shalt raise up the foundations of many generations; and thou shalt be called, The repairer of the breach, The restorer of paths to dwell in (Isaiah 58:12).

What are the waste places? The areas of desolation?

They are the pits -- problems, troubles, tribulations - we experience in our lives.

The Hebrews called the areas left after the ravages of war the *waste places* -- places of desolation left in ruin by the forces of hell. Demon powers freely operate in the midst of these desolate pits.

God is ready to wreck havoc in the corridors of hell for the glory of God!

But who are those that shall be of thee?

They are the church, the ecclesia, the called out ones.

God is saying to the church in this final hour, "All those that are of me, go build on these waste places. Restore the homes and rebuild the lives the devil has ravaged and plundered. Show those in desolation and despair the road to the palace. Show them my plan and my purpose."

Church, get ready to loose the captives and set them free.

Get ready to heal the sick, to raise the dead, to cast out devils and bring His Kingdom to this earth!

His Vision is NOT Man-made!

Most Christians do not comprehend the magnitude of God's vision for their destiny because we do not have many modern-day prophets. Instead, we have pulpiteers who are content to attend their church board meetings and make their man made plans. Too much of the church is satisfied living an idolatrous lifestyle, and worshiping an image of the god that their lifestyle dictates!

But we are only going to destroy the forces of hell and begin to walk in signs, wonders and miracles when we become obedient to the plan and purpose of God.

Receive the Vision

For too long we have been satisfied with the knowledge of someone else's revelation of God. It is time we climbed the mountain peaks of the glory of God, breathed the air of His presence, and allowed Him to reveal Himself to us. Come up to the place where you can see Him, know Him and experience Him for yourself.

Do you want to know Him?

Are you looking for the God whom your soul loves?

I am putting hell on red alert. The church of the living God is alive and well! His people know His plan; they're not taking up residence in the pit. In this final hour of spiritual history, we are a church making ready to follow the vision all the way to His palace!

Get ready, because God is about to do something in your life that hell cannot stop and the storms of life cannot quench!

But if any provide not for his own, and specially for those of his own house, he hath denied the faith, and is worse than an infidel (1 Timothy 5:8).

CHAPTER FOUR

Fathers in the Palace

If you want to be part of God's endtime vision, you must be willing to be made a "spectacle unto the world" for the cause of Christ.

For I think that God hath set forth us the apostles last, as it were appointed to death: for we are made a spectacle unto the world, and to angels, and to men.

We are fools for Christ's sake, but ye are wise in Christ; we are weak, but ye are strong; ye are honourable, but we are despised (1 Corinthians 4:9,10).

When God allowed Job to walk through the pit, his friends and relatives laughed and mocked him for remaining faithful to his Lord. Even Job's own wife urged him to curse God and end the misery of his existence.

Job replied to his mockers, "Go ahead and laugh, but I have been in the mountain. I have seen Him. I have heard His voice rolling in my spirit. Even in the midst of adversity, even in the pit, I know His plan!"

Even unto this present hour we both hunger, and thirst, and are naked, and are buffeted, and have no certain dwellingplace; And labour, working with our own hands: being reviled, we bless; being persecuted, we suffer it (1 Corinthians 4:11,12).

The same spirit that was in Job continued in the apostles. Though they were hungry and thirsty and had no permanent home, they suffered it as a blessing!

In the midst of the pit, Paul continued faithfully to serve God.

Being defamed, we intreat: we are made as the filth of the world and are the offscouring of all things unto this day. I write not these things to shame you, but as my beloved sons I warn you.

For though ye have ten thousand instructors in Christ yet have ye not many fathers: for in Christ Jesus I have begotten you through the gospel (1 Corinthians 4:13-15).

We have many different voices today trying to lead us to the vision. But God is not looking for Bible instructors. He is looking for those who are willing to become fathers, fools for Christ, those who are not fearful of being defamed and persecuted.

These are not popular ideas. You will not have to wait in a long line to volunteer for this duty!

No one likes to hear that the pit may be God's will for them while their relatives and friends laugh and mock at them. But it is a father's responsibility to teach his children, even if it means allowing them to experience some personal hardship to learn the lesson.

Most instructors of the Gospel will not tell you this. If you turn on your local Christian television station, you will hear every doctrine known to man. Seldom will these doctrines relate to the real vision of God.

You will be told "Jesus is coming," and "Jesus is never coming."

You will be informed that "it takes the blood to be saved." Another equally eloquent instructor will tell you "you don't need the blood for salvation."

After a few hours of hearing these myriad doctrines of man, you will be as confused as a mouse in a maze.

But God has revealed a vision that will get you to the palace! He has placed a sovereign institution on this planet for the protection and maturing of His people ... and it is called the church!

I will build my church; and the gates of hell shall not prevail against it (Matthew 16:18).

"Well, Brother Rod, I'm in a church, but the devil sure seems to be prevailing in my life. I am being knocked down and troubled. My kid is on crack. I don't know where to turn. I don't have a dollar to change. I am worried when I get up and worried when I go to bed. My life really is in the pit."

If your life is one defeat after another...

If you are in a sink hole that seems so deep you'll never get out, you are in the wrong place ... at the wrong time ... with the wrong people ... and the wrong vision!

Where there is no vision, the people perish (Proverb 29:18).

When you are under the protection of God's provision for the ecclesia, then the gates of hell will not prevail against you.

That is God's promise to His people.

There has been a great deal of discussion concerning the man who will not provide for his family. The head of the home provides his family with a home to live in, food on the table and clothes for their bodies.

But Paul is not writing about the nuclear family here!

Paul is discussing the household of faith and addressing the shepherding fathers of that household -- the pastor of the local church body.

Sometimes, the local body is led by what Scripture calls an *infidel* -- someone who is ruled and dominated by his physical senses (what he hears, sees, tastes, touches, feels and smells.)

But if any provide not for his own, and specially for those of his own house, he hath denied the faith, and is worse than an infidel (1 Timothy 5:8).

Paul understood that those ruled by their senses only operate in the natural realm. It is impossible for them to receive a revelation of Christ because that can only come through the spiritual, or supernatural realm.

What could possibly be worse than someone totally dominated by his senses?

An infidel will send himself to hell. But an infidel standing behind a pulpit will not only send himself to hell, he will take with him a boxcar load of those he has been charged to provide for and to protect.

Worse than infidels, they are ruled by what the board thinks or what the denominational headquarters thinks or what they see with their senses.

Worse than an infidel!

Pray that pastors will not rule as infidels. Pray they will not be ruled by what they see or motivated by what they hear and touch. Pray that the leaders of our churches will spend time with God in the spirit and receive a vision not born from their senses. Pray for God's anointing of prophetic voices to lovingly lead their sheep along the path to the palace.

The Church today desperately needs some John the Baptists coming out of the wilderness, eating locusts and wild honey, saying "I'm not ruled by my senses! I'm steering the ship of Zion by the Holy Spirit that dwells within me!"

There are too many religious institutions where men have chosen to place God's name on their works without first seeking His vision.

How can you know where God has placed His name?

And these signs shall follow them that believe; In my name shall they cast out devils; they shall speak with new tongues;

They shall take up serpents; and if they drink any deadly thing, it shall not hurt them; they shall lay hands on the sick, and they shall recover (Mark 16:17,18).

The Father Has Foreknowledge

What kind of provision does the visionary of the household of faith provide?

He is a loving shepherd to the flock.

What does that mean?

It means he goes before you because he knows what lies ahead. He has foreknowledge; he knows God's plan.

The pastor who has been given care over the household of faith receives the direction of God. A visionary does not call a meeting of the church board and ask them for direction. He does not call the largest financial donor into his office and say, "What do you think we should do about the next building program?"

He already knows what God has laid on His heart for every situation before it comes to pass! Foreknowledge is born from the heart and is for provision, protection and care for those of that house.

The pastor who has heard the voice of God does not know what he knows because of something he saw on television or because of a plan he saw work for someone else.

If you are the father to a family of believers, do not be satisfied with someone else's revelation! Leaders, individually, receive the vision. They pay the price in prayer, fasting, meditation and study. They draw away from the world and into the presence of God. They spend time in praise, adoration and worship until they receive His direction.

The Vision Speaks!

For the vision is yet for an appointed time, but at the end it shall speak, and not lie (Habakkuk 2:3).

Those to whom God has placed His name may be buffeted in battle but they will NEVER fail!

The vision, birthed from the spirit, produces protection, provision and care on the road to the palace.

Where there is no vision, the people perish (Proverbs 29:18).

The foreknowledge of the vision protects us!

You are part of the foreknowledge of God's vision and have a part to play in it. God foreknew the attacks of the enemy in your life, watched over you in the pit, and He has already revealed to you what the end result will be ... **if** you have sought His face!

It does not matter what happens between A and Z. God has already declared you are going to make it all the way to Z, and He intends for you to dwell in the palace!

The Senses are Non-Sense!

It does not matter what your situation looks like. It does not matter how cold your pit is or how deep it seems to go.

You are predestined for the palace in the plan and purpose of God.

God foreknew, and because He foreknew, He predestined.

You are predestined as royalty for the palace!

Predestination means it has already come to pass in the mind and heart of God. The devil cannot affect your tomorrow any more than he can do anything about your yesterday!

Do you see the protection of the vision?

Fear is false evidence that appears real.

You only fear what you do not know.

Once you know the outcome of your struggles, there

is nothing left to fear!

Foreknowledge is Spirit Knowledge

Spiritual knowledge transcends intellectual knowledge, and intellectual knowledge transcends sense knowledge.

Sense knowledge is the lowest form of knowledge. Your senses will lie to you, because your body is still under the curse.

Mental knowledge can dominate sense knowledge, but because it is not redeemed it will lie to you as well. Your mind can trick your body. Just start telling yourself how bad you feel, and it will not take very long before your muscles are aching.

You can go to all the schools of higher learning, but you will never obtain true knowledge through secular education ... it is not redeemed!

Spirit knowledge is revelation knowledge, and it allows you to flow in the vision! When you are sanctified by His blood, you walk in His knowledge.

You are perfected in knowledge that flows from the Spirit of God ... not in your body, not in your mind, not in your will or your emotions ... but in your spirit!

Living in the palace means living a life in the spirit!

The only part of man's being that did not come from the earthiness of this planet is his spirit -- that came from

God. Your spirit is perfect and will never lie to you.

Learn to walk in the spirit and God will provide for the needs of your life!

The Spiritual Shepherd

God provides BEFORE you have a need!

In ancient times, the shepherd dipped the heads of the sheep in vats of oil before they went out to graze. He knew that while the sheep grazed on the stubble around the rocky terrain of Jerusalem, they often cut their heads on the rocks. Since the shepherd could not possibly be near every sheep when they were cut, he made provision for their needs -- before they were ever injured!

BEFORE the rocks and brambles could cut the sheep, he had already provided for their safety.

The shepherd knew that an open wound under the blazing desert sun could cost the sheep its life. It could easily become infected before he could ever get to it with medical aid. So, he put the oil on in advance. The oil was already in the wool, ready to run down into the wound if the sheep was cut on the rocks.

If you want protection on the road to the palace, travel under the vision of the household of faith and walk out the prophetic Word of God in your life.

Sickness will melt from your body.

Physical pains will leave.

The blessing of God will follow you.

He is our Jehovah Jireh. He is the God who provides -- IN ADVANCE -- before there is a need.

He made a planet with grass on it before He made cows who needed to eat it. And He has made provision for you to make it through the pit and end up at the pre-appointed destination, the palace.

Where there is no vision,
the people perish
(Proverb 29:18).

CHAPTER FIVE

Protection from the Pit!

Vision means receiving a prophetic utterance.

Where there is no prophetic voice of God to direct and correct, the people wallow and perish in the pit!

Where there is no prophetic voice, there are only the meaningless motions of man, preaching from the mind to receive the accolades of others.

Where there is no prophetic voice, the flock flounders in the pit of confusion.

The church needs visionaries who will stand behind a pulpit and declare, "I have seen Him that your soul desires, and here is how you can get out of the pit and dwell in the palace with Him."

The prophetic voice will take you from where you are to where you want to be in God!

Prophets point the way from the pit to the palace.

The church is yearning to march to the prophetic voice and anointing of God to bring about His will in the earth, but the people are running scattered.

Jesus was moved to compassion when He saw crowds without direction.

And Jesus, when he came out, saw much people, and was moved with compassion toward them, because they were as sheep not having a shepherd (Mark 6:34).

It is the shepherd's responsibility to provide protection within the house of God.

There is a wall of protection inside prophetic direction that keeps the body from running its own way.

God is doing something ... NOW!!

Christ is walking among His people, moving by His Spirit ... drawing, wooing, forming, cutting away, planting in, tearing out, rooting out, building and establishing.

The church has reached adolescence and is on its way to adulthood. The church is coming out of the pit and is headed for the palace.

One Prophetic Voice

Imagine the devil's agony when God's children come together under the sacred unity of the prophetic voice of

God because they know there is protection and provision in God's house! Inside the scope of the vision of God's house, there is security.

Come away from the adolescent idea that the shepherd in the church is only asking us to follow his little parade. If a leader is a true visionary, it is not his parade; it is our parade.

It is not his vision, it is our vision.

It is not his palace, it is our palace.

God's church, united together as His body, will bring His will to pass.

The church is not an evangelistic center, a convention center or a seminar center. The local church represents the universal body of Christ, blessed by God to implement His purpose and His plan!

Spiritual Moat

In His vision, there is protection.

Moats were built around palaces for protection. They were a line of defense from the enemy.

When the church operates in God's vision, a spiritual moat encircles the entire body. It is a hedge of protection that the devil cannot cross!

Stay in His vision and you will walk under the protection of the shadow of the Almighty!

The people of God yearn to know the boundaries and

the direction of the vision. They long to hear His voice. His children come into His presence and discern His direction. They are not slaves to their senses, but receive direction born in prayer.

We MUST respond to His voice. We cannot treat the Word of God spoken from the pulpit as if it was an announcement for the next church social. The pastor speaks with the voice of God, revealing the plan and the purpose of God.

A divine wave is sweeping the earth, announcing the prophetic direction of God. If we will be obedient to the word spoken forth, we can ride the crest of the wave all the way to the palace. But if we disobey, trying to bring natural plans and purposes to pass, that thundering wave of the power of God will crush us.

Vision Produces Restraint!

Where there is no prophetic word going forth under the anointing of God, the people cast off restraint. The people do not know what to do, where to go, or how to walk. A prophetic anointing produces the boldness to instruct and guide the flock without fear of driving them into another pasture.

The people of God hate evil and love righteousness. The people of God hate the works of darkness. They refuse to settle for the darkness of the pit, and hunger for the light.

Vision is the foreknowledge, and the hedge of protection that surrounds the people, and it is time to make the prophetic vision clear.

The people of God are not resisting the voice of God; they are just not hearing it!

There is so much pabulum spewing from the pulpits Christians cannot hear the prophetic voice of God.

The vision is the boundary of protection that completely surrounds the palace. It says, "Go this far and do this, but do not go that far and do not do that." Boundaries unite the church and bring it to life.

If you live your life in the vision, you will receive the anointing of God. You will receive power to preach the Gospel and set the captives free.

If you cast off restraint, your self-will will produce pride. Your pride will, in turn, produce a fall.

Churches without the vision have the same divorce rate as the world. Racism blazes like an open bonfire. People sit in their cozy pews on Sunday and devour pornography on Monday.

Where there is no vision, the people cast off restraint and go their own way. They wallow in the pitfalls of a world gone mad. They become self-willed, full of pride and walk away from the things of God.

But when God delivers His prophetic word to those who know His voice, the people bow their heads and say,

"Great is the Lord and worthy to be praised."

I hear the swords clashing as the body of Christ draws them from their sheaths. The church is making ready to march under the orders of the heavenly commander-in-chief. But is anyone there to give them the vision?

Write the vision, and make it plain (Habbakuk 2:2).

Obedience Brings Provision

And Elijah the Tishbite, who was of the inhabitants of Gilead, said unto Ahab, As the Lord God of Israel liveth, before whom I stand, there shall not be dew nor rain these years, but according to my word (1 Kings 17:1).

The man of God stood before the king and declared, "There will be no rain until I say so." Elijah recognized that God had given him dominion over everything -- even the rain!

And the word of the Lord came unto him, saying, Get thee hence, and turn thee eastward, and hide thyself by the brook Cherith, that is before Jordan.

And it shall be, that thou shalt drink of the brook; and I have commanded the ravens to feed thee there (1 Kings 17:2-4).

The Lord gave His prophet very specific instructions and then commanded the ravens to feed him. Elijah's obedience to the Lord's instructions unlocked the door of provision for the miraculous. Elijah received the vision of the

Lord, and as he obeyed ... God provided.

And the ravens brought him bread and flesh in the morning, and bread and flesh in the evening; and he drank of the brook (v.6).

As Elijah trusted God, the Lord released His provision into the prophet's life.

Today, some of us trust the church instead of the God of the church. Some of us trust the preacher more than the God of the preacher. Some of us trust in the prayer rather than the God behind the prayer.

Trust the Word of God and He will confirm it! Where the Word of God goes forth and the vision of God is made clear, He pours forth His anointing to bring it to pass.

God is saying, "I will not disappoint you or leave you empty-handed. It was my Word that said you would be fed by the brook, and I am obligated to my Word! I will meet you at the point of your need when you obey my Word."

Later, Elijah is instructed to journey to Zarephath and look for a widow woman.

Arise, get thee to Zarephath, which belongeth to Zidon, and dwell there: behold, I have commanded a widow woman there to sustain thee.

So he arose and went to Zarephath. And when he came to the gate of the city, behold, the widow woman was there gathering of sticks: and he called to her, and said, Fetch me, I pray thee, a little water in a vessel, that I may drink (vv. 9,10).

She obeyed the man of God, even though water was the most precious commodity in her town. She ignored the cost and made the sacrifice.

Miracles through Obedience

Miracles come not by works but by grace.

The palace is ours not by works but by grace!

The manifold wisdom of God is released on this earth by grace. It is not released because we are so wonderful, because of what we do, not because of our confessions, our daily penances or because we pray great swelling words. The wisdom of God is released through absolute obedience to the Word of God!

He sees our obedience and says, "They are going after my Word. They are doing my Word regardless of the cost to them. I am obligated to perform my Word on their behalf!"

It is that simple. Listen for His Word through His prophets and obey that Word.

Be willing to sacrifice your time, your talent and your material possessions if you really desire to live in the palace with Him.

And as she was going to fetch it, he called to her, and said, Bring me, I pray thee, a morsel of bread in thine hand.

And she said, As the Lord thy God liveth, I have not a cake, but an handful of meal in a barrel, and a little oil in a cruse: and behold, I am gathering two sticks, that I may go in and dress it for me and my son, that we may eat it, and die (vv. 11,12).

The poor little widow could not see the miracle God had in store for her; but, despite her circumstances, she walked in obedience to the prophet.

Although she did not understand B through Y, she had a vision of A and Z and believed God for the rest.

This woman needed a miracle to escape starvation.

Elijah said unto her, *Fear not (1 Kings 17:13).*

Jesus said the same two words to His disciples on that storm-tossed sea, to blind Bartimaeus, to the woman taken in adultery, to the lepers and to Peter.

He was saying, "Fear not, little flock, for the outcome of this situation is predestined. You are not destined to set up residence in these pits; you're going to live in the palace. Your Heavenly Father has already made the provision."

The Price of the Vision

Unity in the body will cause the Spirit of the Lord to rend the heavens and come down in demonstration of His unleashed, omnipotent power.

But to come together in the vision is going to cost

us something.

It will cost us identity.

It will cost our ideas.

It is going to mean putting aside our man made church programs and replacing them with the vision of God.

Behold, how good and how pleasant it is for brethren to dwell together in unity!

It is like the precious ointment upon the head, that ran down upon the beard, even Aaron's beard: that went down to the skirts of his garments (Psalm 133:1,2).

Unity is a *precious ointment,* and it will unleash the anointing.

The yoke shall be destroyed because (or in the presence) of the anointing (Isaiah 10:27).

God said, "I will command my anointing, and that anointing will destroy every single yoke of bondage."

What is the anointing?

It is the eternal power of God that breaks through every line of Satan's defense and propels you from the pit to the palace.

For the word of God is quick, and powerful, and sharper than any two-edged sword, piercing even to the dividing asunder of soul and spirit, and of the joints and marrow, and is a discerner of the thoughts and intents of the heart (Hebrews 4:12).

CHAPTER SIX

Children of Royal Destiny

How we receive His Word reflects our heart.

When His Word comes, we either respond in obedience or disobedience, and by our response to that Word our heart is revealed to God.

It is not enough to acknowledge our blessings. If we are not changed by His Word -- if it hasn't made a difference in our lives -- it has fallen on barren ground.

Palace Living

As a royal heir to the kingdom, you must prepare for palace living.

How? Through adoration and worship.

Adoration is the purist form of worship, where we are

not singing and shouting His praises ... but instead can do nothing except lay prostrate in His presence. Abandon yourself until there is nothing left of you and everything of Him.

Pray for Him to release His cleansing, refining, purifying power in your life, as you become broken bread and poured out wine in a lifestyle of adoration of who He is. Pray that your heart responds as an instrument of praise in every task you set your hand to, as you walk out His will in your life.

Fresh Fire

For too many, the first experience in baptism in the Holy Ghost is their last. If we have not had an experience with God today, we are late. If we did not receive a fresh baptism yesterday, we are behind.

Some are wallowing around in yesterday's ashes. But God said, *And the priest shall put on his linen garment, and his linen breeches shall he put upon his flesh, and take up the ashes which the fire hath consumed with the burnt offering on the altar, and he shall put them beside the altar. And he shall put off his garments, and put on other garments, and carry forth the ashes without the camp unto a clean place (Leviticus 6:10,11).*

He is saying, "Take yesterday's ashes off the altar and get them out of my presence!"

To dwell in the celestial heights of the palace requires fresh fire every day! Prostrate yourself before Him and say, "I am not ready to go forth in power until I have first been touched by you."

Dwelling in the palace requires fresh oil every day. That oil then pours down from the altar of God and spills over our lives like molten gold. We need an experience with God that moves us to cry, "He is our life; in Him we live, and move and have our being! Unless He is manifested in us, we dare not move at all!"

Demonstrate the Vision

Once we start walking in the vision, we will begin to experience the manifestation of the gifts of the Spirit.

Not only has the prophetic voice been too silent, the church has been too weak to demonstrate His power through the gifts of the Holy Spirit.

The endtime revival will come on the wings of the gifts of the Holy Ghost. Tongues; the interpretation of tongues; prophecy; the word of wisdom; the word of knowledge; the discerning of spirits; wonder-working faith; the gifts of healing; and the working of miracles will explode in power in the last days for the mighty harvest of souls before the tribulation comes (I Corinthians 12:7-11).

The local church is a representation of the whole body of Christ. Whatever composes the universal church, the entire church of Jesus Christ, should also be part of the local church. In His church there are apostles, prophets, evangelists, pastors and teachers working in unity with one goal, one purpose, one vision, one Lord, one baptism ... all with the same focus (Ephesians 4:4-13).

God is raising up local churches in America where every service will manifest the apostle, the prophet, the evangelist, the pastor and the teacher. They will be set in the church in three groups and will come and go: 1) those set permanently in the local assembly who rarely, if ever, go out; 2) those primarily set in but who are used outside the local setting; and 3) those who mainly travel beyond the local assembly but who are very strongly tied into it. They will all be joined together with the local church where they receive their strength.

The reason we do not see a greater manifestation of the evangelistic gift today is because the people are wandering away from the covering of the local church. Too often we flounder in the pit because we are not yielded to local church leadership. Every person I know who is being used by the Spirit of God in this endtime hour is tied into the authority of a local church!

Through our own petty sins, we have deprived ourselves of many of the fivefold ministry gifts. Many apostles and prophets cannot abide together in the same house without becoming jealous of one another's gifts. We need pastors and teachers who can rise above petty jealousies and allow each other to operate in their callings without causing divisions in the body.

The time for the prophetic voice of God has come. He is looking for a people who will say "yes and amen" to the vision. God is looking for men who will declare, "I am nothing and you are everything. Have your way, Lord! Take me from the pit to the palace."

God is about His work in spite of us. He is moving us out of the way. He has said, "You prayed that I would have my way and I intend on having it."

Action Under the Vision

You are a living miracle.

Do what God said to do.

Champion the cause of Christ.

When the visionary anointing is released in your life, you begin to march under the vision of the palace. You rise up every morning declaring, "God, I expect to have a revelation of you today that I did not have yesterday. I am seeking your Word. I will do everything I can do to receive it."

"I will adore you in my lifestyle today, and I expect a fresh baptism in the Holy Ghost to cause me to operate in your gifts."

Destiny's Children

We are destined to experience the manifestation and revelation of the glory of God!

We are perfected in the Spirit, but our soulish man is renewed through the Word of God.

I beseech you therefore, brethren, by the mercies of God, that ye present your bodies a living sacrifice, holy, acceptable unto God, which is your reasonable service.

And be not conformed to this world: but be ye transformed by the renewing of your mind (Romans 12:1,2).

God has more planned for you than just sitting in a church pew and "amening" the pastor. You are holy royalty ... destined for the palace! You are a child of the King, and you are created for signs and wonders!

A wonder is the mighty miracle-working power of God that extends beyond our natural ability to even think or ask for it. We are serving a God who is super-abundantly able to perform all that we ask or think, so do not be afraid to ask Him.

In fact, He commands you to ask Him.

Ask, and it shall be given you; seek, and ye shall find; knock, and it shall be opened to you (Matthew 7:7).

While much of the church is still learning to ask, God has a people who are past the asking and seeking the supply of God. God has a people ready to rend the heavens and do things above and beyond what they are even able to ask or think in the natural realm!

That is a wonder.

For though we walk in the flesh, we do not war after the flesh:

(For the weapons of our warfare are not carnal, but mighty through God to the pulling down of strong holds) (2 Corinthians 10:3,4).

Supernatural Royalty

We are supernatural.

Super means *more than.* You are more than natural.

You have been destined to soar on the wings of the supernatural, to see the supernatural, to be the supernatural and to do the supernatural.

You are supernatural royalty and destined to be a sign and a wonder to a lost and hurting world!

Afterward he appeared unto the eleven as they sat at meat, and upbraided them with their unbelief and hardness of heart, because they believed not them which had seen him after he was risen.

And he said unto them, Go ye into all the world, and preach the Gospel to every creature.

He that believeth and is baptized shall be saved; but he that believeth not shall be damned.

And these signs shall follow them that believe; In my name shall they cast out devils; they shall speak with new tongues (Mark 16:14-17).

Do you see it?

You are destined to experience the manifested, tangible presence of God.

They shall take up serpents; and if they drink any deadly thing, it shall not hurt them; they shall lay hands on the sick and they shall recover.

So then after the Lord had spoken unto them, he was received up into heaven, and sat on the right hand of God.

And they went forth, and preached every where, the Lord working with them, and confirming the word with signs following. Amen (Mark 16:18-20).

Miracles are sign posts from God, valuable not so much for what they are as for what they reveal about the grace and power of Almighty God. God has a people destined to reach into the realm of the spirit and pull the miraculous into the natural ... to manifest the demonstration, the tangibility, the purpose and the destiny of Almighty God.

God is pouring out His Spirit on all flesh. He wants to place His healing power in your hands to confirm His Word and give new assurance that His Word is still valid and relevant today.

People have no problem believing that Jesus of Nazareth wiped the blindness from Bartimaeus' eyes. But they tumble headlong into the pit of doubt and unbelief when it comes to healing their bodies today.

"It is wonderful," they say, "that Jesus healed Bartimaeus' eyes; but what about these cataracts on my own eyes?"

God, in His predestination and forethought -- in His plan and purpose -- said, "I will make something available that lets people know on a daily basis that my Word was valid for Bartimaeus, and it is valid where they are today. I will do signs and wonders to give assurance of the validity of my Word!"

We serve a now Jesus.

We serve a water-walking Jesus today.

We serve a blind-man healing, leper-cleansing man today. Through signs and wonders, we are destined to manifest the vision of God, in the name of the Lord!

Palace People Produce the Proof

God's palace people will remove all doubt about the claims of Jesus. We will produce the proof of His message by performing the same indisputable, skeptic-silencing acts of spiritual authority Jesus performed in His own day.

Acts 1:8 declares, *But ye shall receive power, after that the Holy Ghost is come upon you.*

God's plan has destined us to receive a supernatural infusion of extraordinary power through the gifts of the

Spirit.

You shall receive power.

That word *power* as translated from the Greek in this passage is the word *dunamis*, meaning *miracle-working ability.*

After that the Holy Ghost is come upon you: and you shall be witnesses unto me both in Jerusalem, and in all Judaea, and in Samaria, and unto the uttermost part of the earth (Acts 1:8).

A witness is one who produces evidence bearing on the truth. If you are a witness, you are an evidence carrier. God said you would be witnesses and give the evidence. The Gospel has not been preached until there are attesting miracles, signs and wonders.

When John the Baptist was in prison he sent out messengers, instructing them to ask the man from Nazareth if He really was the one, or should they look for another?

Jesus answered,

The blind receive their sight, and the lame walk, the lepers are cleansed, and the deaf hear, the dead are raised up, and the poor have the gospel preached to them (Matthew 11:5).

He was saying, "I have produced the evidence. Yes, I am the one!"

Jesus' ministry manifested signs and wonders.

Jesus' message was enforced by demonstration --

evidence that He was who He said He was.

The same is true of the followers of Jesus.

And the people with one accord gave heed unto those things which Philip spake, hearing and seeing the miracles which he did (Acts 8:6).

Philip preached and people listened.

The entire unbelieving city of Samaria was turned around. They heeded Philip's words not because he went to a seminary, or headed a church, or was on television, or knew someone who knew someone. They paid attention to Philip because of the signs and wonders they saw and because of the powerful Word that came forth. Philip was preaching with confirmation and attesting with signs, wonders and miracles!

How can you recognize the followers of Jesus? Through signs, wonders, miracles and the gifts of the Holy Ghost.

How can we know if the local church is flowing in the anointing of the Spirit of God? Through signs, wonders, miracles and the gifts of the Holy Ghost. They are the evidence!

Every morning ask God for signs, wonders, miracles and gifts of the Holy Ghost. They are a sure sign of palace people, supernatural royalty living in the palace.

For I determined not to know any thing among you, save Jesus Christ, and him crucified.

And I was with you in weakness, and in fear, and in much trembling. And my speech and my preaching was not with enticing words of man's wisdom, but in demonstration of the Spirit and of power:

That your faith should not stand in the wisdom of men, but in the power of God (1 Corinthians 2:2-5).

The Purpose of Miracles

God manifests miracles for five reasons:

1. To establish the claims of Christ

Jesus said, *If I do not the works of my Father, believe me not (John 10:37).* Miracles prove Jesus was who He said He was and, more importantly, is who He says He is.

2. To establish faith in the resurrection

When Peter and John were at the temple gate they said,

Silver and gold have I none; but such as I have give I thee: In the name of Jesus Christ of Nazareth rise up and walk (Acts 3:6).

The Word of God declares, *And with great power gave the apostles witness of the resurrection of the Lord Jesus (Acts 4:33).*

3. To attract the lost to the Gospel

Jesus healed more sinners than He did saints because miracles attract people.

4. To turn sinners to God

When Peter met a man who had been sick with the palsy for eight years, he said to him, *Jesus Christ maketh thee whole: arise, and make thy bed (Acts 9:34).*

The man immediately rose from his bed healed, and the entire city was saved. *And all that dwelt at Lydda and Saron saw him, and turned to the Lord (Acts 9:35).*

5. To confirm the Gospel

How shall we escape, if we neglect so great salvation; which at the first began to be spoken by the Lord, and was confirmed unto us by them that heard him;

God also bearing them witness, both with signs and wonders, and with divers miracles and gifts of the Holy Ghost, according to his own will? (Hebrews 2:3,4).

Receive His Miracle-Working Power!

We have been given the biblical formula to receiving God's miracle-working power in Luke 1:26-41 and in Luke 2:5-6 which is the story of Mary and the conception of Jesus. Certain keys emerge from these passages.

Key #1: To experience a miracle, you must receive a Word from God.

And the angel came in unto her, and said, Hail, thou that art highly favoured, the Lord is with thee: blessed art thou among women ... And, behold, thou shalt conceive in thy womb, and bring forth a son, and shalt call his name JESUS (Luke 1:28,31).

Key #2: Stay preserved.

Some cannot receive miracles because they are so full of the husks of the world.

If you could see in the spirit, you would discover all the aborted miracles God was ready to give birth to, laying in mounds of deadened hopelessness.

Why? Because God's palace dwellers lost the vision. They fell into doubt, unbelief, murmuring, complaining and gossiping.

Miracles come through seeking the Word of God.

When the refuse of a worldly life dedicated to fleshly indulgences infringes upon what God wants as virginal territory, it must be cast off! That is why, when Jesus entered the room where the little girl lay dead, He ordered all the unbelievers from the room. Jesus wanted nothing to contaminate the miracle waiting for that young girl (Mark 5:35-43).

Key #3: Accept God's methods.

Mary accepted God's plan, even though it meant potential embarrassment in her community. She accepted His direction and did not argue with His divine plan for her life. Not once did she say, "Lord, what are the people going to think?"

Today, as a royal heir, God wants to impregnate you with your heritage.

Key #4: Cast out all fear.

100

Get rid of anything that is antagonistic to your seed. Do not allow any element of fear to interfere with God's plan for your life.

For God hath not given us the spirit of fear; but of power, and of love, and of a sound mind (2 Timothy 1:7).

Key #5: Wait for the vision.

It will come. Just as in a natural pregnancy, miracles have a spiritual gestation period. During this stage be thankful that you know it is finished and the miracle is on the way!

Royal Security

Walking in the miracles of God and faithfulness to His vision protects us from the ravaging forces of hell. Our submission to God's royal plan, covered by the blood of Jesus, is the only thing that will kick cancer out of our bodies. It will rescue our kids from crack, put the healing power of God back into our hands and return the glory of God to the church.

Follow the vision ... it will lead you to the palace.

Go into the highways and the byways, heal the sick, cast out devils, cleanse the lepers, raise the dead, share the Gospel to those who are lost. Become a witness to others that God came down from heaven in the form of His Son, died on a cross, rose from the dead, is coming again and can still save the lowest sinner!

God's vision for each of us is to share the REAL GOSPEL, not the gospels of self-help, compromise and innuendo. Where there is no vision of the REAL GOSPEL, the people perish.

Tell others that there is a purpose to the pit.

Tell others that God may allow a season of trial and tribulation ... but He has a plan.

And tell them that despite their trials, despite their time in the pit ... God knows them, sees them, loves them and has a plan which calls for them to ultimately dwell in the palace with Him.

Where there is no prophetic voice of truth ... the people perish.

Share the REAL Gospel with signs and wonders -- they are not optional.

Jesus said, *The Spirit of the Lord is upon me, because he hath anointed me to preach the gospel to the poor; he hath sent me to heal the brokenhearted, to preach deliverance to the captives, and recovering of sight to the blind, to set at liberty them that are bruised, to preach the acceptable year of the Lord (Luke 4:18,19).*

That is the vision.

It has not changed!

Plain Palace Living
Write the vision, and make it plain upon tables, that he may run that readeth it (Habakkuk 2:2).

God has made His vision plain on tables with the fiery finger of the Holy Ghost. God has taken His Word and branded it on our spirit, and now it is time for us to *run*.

You have the vision for the palace, and that vision contains protection and anointing to destroy every yoke!

Behold, I and the children whom the Lord hath given me are for signs and for wonders (Isaiah 8:18).

As a royal child of His Majesty, the King, you are part of a triumphant, victorious, blood-bought, fire-baptized remnant church of Jesus Christ. Rest in that place of supernatural protection. You are surrounded by a hedge of protection, and the devil cannot harm you.

Your pit cannot change your destiny!

Even if you are in the pit today, whether it is the pit of addiction, perversion, homosexuality, sickness or destroyed relationships ... God has already provided your answer!

You are destined for the palace!

It does not matter if you have had an abortion, committed murder, or spent time in jail. The Gospel of Jesus Christ was predestined to set you free, and He that the Son sets free is free indeed!

Defeated Devils Behind Cardboard Gates
Hell is occupied by defeated devils.

The gates of hell are made of crushed cardboard.

The church of Jesus Christ is a blazing torch loosed against the flimsy facade of the gates of hell! They cannot hold you back from what God has destined for you.

If you are in the pit right now, God is telling you, "Do not be concerned about the fiery trials that try to destroy your faith. You know the end result, and it brings a great reward."

You are destined to dwell victoriously in the palace ... in healing, in finances, in family relationships, in addictions and in every other form of bondage known to man!

God has ultimately predestinated you to be at Z ... where healing, victory, health, deliverance, provision, protection, plenty, peace and power reside.

You are royalty.

God predestined you for a victorious life, and there is nothing the devil can do to keep you from ending up there ... as long as you stay in the vision.

Only when you step out from under the covering of the vision, through disobedience, can the devil bring his destruction.

Where there are those speaking from the Spirit of God and not their own spirit, there is a wall of protection that surrounds the people.

Half Visions
Much of the church today has only half the vision of

the palace.

Half of the vision is the message, the other half is the miracles that prove the message. A message without miracles is dead religion and philosophy. Miracles without a message are not rooted and grounded in the Word, and cause the people to run wild in emotionalism.

If America is ever going to be saved, it will be through a church flowing in both the message of the cross and the miracle of the resurrection!

Miracles are not optional ... they are the evidence that we are children of the King! It is not optional for you to lay hands on the sick, to cast out devils and to believe for miracles.

Do miracles follow you? Are you asking for them? The Bible says you have not because you ask not (John 16:24).

If you ask, know with steadfast confidence and assurance that you have granted to you for your present possession whatever it is that you ask Him for. God is going to find a vessel through which His power will flow to meet every need, to break every bondage.

That is the vision of the palace!

The Spirit of the Lord God is upon me; because the Lord hath anointed me to preach good tidings unto the meek; he hath sent me to bind up the brokenhearted, to proclaim liberty to the captives, and the opening of the prison to them that are bound (Isaiah 61:1).

The vision is freedom.

The vision is miracles.

The New Testament is full of this vision! There is a dying world and a risen Savior, and you and I are the miracle link between the two!

You are a keg of dynamite primed to explode against the gates of hell. You have been predestined to dwell in the palace, and your heritage as a royal child of God is to end up in victory!

Though he were a Son, yet learned he obedience by the things which he suffered;

And being made perfect, he became the author of eternal salvation unto all them that obey him (Hebrews 5:8,9).

CHAPTER SEVEN

You can LOVE the Pit!

You may be in the pit right now, but you are there with some very good company!

Moses had his time of blessings in the palace, but he also spent time in the pit.

By faith Moses, when he was come to years, refused to be called the son of Pharaoh's daughter; Choosing rather to suffer affliction with the people of God, than to enjoy the pleasures of sin for a season (Hebrews 11:24,25).

Moses chose to live in the midst of affliction rather than compromise himself as a child of God! Although he was God's chosen vessel to lead the Jews out of Israel, for forty years Moses wandered in the wilderness!

At the end of that forty-year stint in the pit ... Moses encountered a burning bush that would not be consumed and heard a heavenly voice.

God told him to "Take off thy shoes from thy feet, for the ground wherein thou standest is holy ground. Moses, you are mine. I have blessed you, and I have also seen you broken. Now, I am ready to take you once again out of the pit and use you in the palace. Go tell the Pharaoh to let my people go." (Exodus 3)

Yes, Moses languished in the pit -- not because God had ignored him, but because God was preparing him for a specific purpose -- to be the deliverer of the house of Israel.

Moving from the pit to the palace is the divine process of God.

David's Exile

What about David?

David was a simple boy who tended his father's sheep in fields near Bethlehem. God sent Samuel to the house of Jesse to anoint one of his sons to be the future king, turned down David's seven older brothers and picked David.

Then Samuel took the horn of oil, and anointed him

in the midst of his brethren: and the Spirit of the Lord came upon David from that day forward. So Samuel rose up, and went to Ramah (1 Samuel 16:13).

Later, this same David slew Goliath and was loved by the people because of it. As a reward, Saul made David captain of his army and gave him his daughter to wed!

Yes, God blessed him; but He allowed David also to languish in the pit. Saul became jealous of David and three times tried to kill him, before David finally fled.

And Saul cast the javelin; for he said, I will smite David even to the wall with it. And David avoided out of his presence twice (1 Samuel 18:11).

For the next several years, David lived as a fugitive, constantly fleeing from place to place trying to avoid Saul. The Bible tells us that David's wife was kidnapped, and there was no one to encourage him during this time of exile.

And David was greatly distressed; for the people spake of stoning him, because the soul of all the people was grieved, every man for his sons and for his daughters: but David encouraged himself in the Lord his God (1 Samuel 30:6).

God was David's only encouragement until his circumstances started to reverse after the death of Saul. Only after David's time of trial, trouble, persecution and preparation did God raise him up and put him in the palace!

And the time that David was king in Hebron over the

house of Judah was seven years and six months (2 Samuel 2:11).

Joseph's Pit

How about Joseph?

God blessed him with special dreams, and because of them his brothers threw him into a pit. When Joseph escaped the pit, he was sold into Egyptian slavery ... where Potiphar's wife unjustly accused Joseph of rape. Because of this charge, Joseph was next tossed into prison.

Can you see the process God uses with His people?

God was saying to Joseph, "First I'll call you; I'll take you for my own. Next I'll bless you to encourage your faith. Then I'll allow you to be broken through the trials where I will prepare you for service in my kingdom."

Jesus Also Suffered

Jesus came to this earth not as an angel but as a man. He came as the seed of Abraham, and God blessed his life.

When Jesus was eight days old, he was taken to the temple to be circumcised. And there was Simeon, standing on the steps of the temple, with tears welling up in his eyes. God told Simeon he would not die until he saw the Messiah. When he beheld the baby boy wrapped in swaddling clothes, this prophet of God, tears streaming down his aging face, announced,

Lord, now lettest thou thy servant depart in peace, according to thy word: for mine eyes have seen thy salvation, which thou hast prepared before the face of all people (Luke 2:29-31).

At age twelve, Jesus astounded His teachers.

Later He walked on water, broke five loaves to feed five thousand men and raised Lazarus from the dead. But after His time of blessing and miracles, you know only too well the rest of the story.

Jesus was required to suffer.

He suffered ... for a purpose!

Though he were a Son, yet learned he obedience by the things which he suffered; and being made perfect, he became the author of eternal salvation unto all them that obey him (Hebrews 5:8,9).

So often I hear Christians say, "Well, if I'd just get really blessed, God would use me." If you only experience blessings, you are not ready to be used! The blessings of God build your faith, but it is in the pit that God allows you to be broken and prepared for service.

Love the Pit!

In my own life I feel I have been to hell and back. I have suffered persecution, ridicule, lies, temptations and trials.

I've seen trouble on every side.

And I'm excited!

Why?

Because I understand God's process.

When you are being dashed on the stones of the trials of life, God is preparing you for service -- He is preparing you for the palace!

God always blesses you first, then comes the breaking as He prepares to bring you forth for service. After a time of blessing, He will allow you to again experience the pit in preparation for the next mighty move to the palace.

That is the divine process He has established!

When that process becomes part of your spirit, you will no longer cry out, "Why me, God?"

Instead, you will cry out, "Lord, thank you for the pit ... thank you for this time of preparation for a new and greater dimension of service to you."

When a wild horse gallops fiercely through an open field it is a beautiful sight, but is serves no purpose. In order for a horse to become useful, it must be broken. The horse has to learn how to operate with a bit in its mouth, controlled by reigns.

The young lady who signs for the deaf in our church was signing as the choir sang, "Our God Reigns." I watched as she gestured as if she were driving a buggy or riding a horse. She was moving her hands back and forth with her forefingers curled, exactly the way I grasp the reins from the bit in a horse's mouth.

You can more fully understand being broken if you realize it is just another step in the process of allowing God to reign in your life. When He reigns, He reins. When He rules, He directs.

When a wild horse is first corralled, it is fed and watered. It no longer has to forage for food; every need is supplied. The owner begins to gain the trust of the animal by providing for it.

God builds you up through blessings, and then He breaks you in the pit as preparation for the next blessing.

When you fully grasp His plan, then you understand how the Word can say,

And we know that all things work together for good to them that love God, to them who are the called according to his purpose (Romans 8:28).

If His purpose for you now means the trial of the fiery furnace, you can submit because you know it is a time of preparation.

If it means you are going to walk into the lion's den, then walk in knowing that God has a purpose for the experience.

You are not forsaken in the trials ... you are loved! The trials are not for punishment ... they are for preparation!

Begin to appreciate your time of trials.

Learn to say,

But now, O Lord, thou art our father; we are the clay, and thou our potter; and we all are the work of thy hand (Isaiah 64:8).

The Devil's Dilemma

What is the devil going to do with a person who embraces the fire, a person who loves the flood, a person who happily endures the darkness of the pit?

That person is you!

You know the process of God, so you love both the blessing and the breaking! You love both the giving and the taking, because you are in the perfect will of God ... all the way from A to Z!

Praise Him ... whether you are in the pit or the palace.

If you are in the palace right now, thank Him for it. But, if you feel your life is in such disarray you do not know where to turn ... praise Him even more!

You are in a time of breaking and preparation!

God will never suffer you to be tempted above that which you can bear, and God intends to use you and your trials as testimonies.

Although you may be in the pit, soon you will be saying, "Yes, I went through the fire, but I don't smell like smoke. I went through the flood, but it didn't overflow me."

When you are in God's will, the devil has no part of

your spirit. Anything that comes into your life, God either sends or He allows. Either way, He will give you the grace to go through it. You will come out the other end ready to do His work for the kingdom.

Maybe you have been mocked.

So was Jesus.

Like Moses ... like David ... like Joseph ... like Jesus ... whether you are in the pit or the palace right now, you are in the divine process and plan of God!

Don't quit.

Don't give up.

Don't turn around.

Hold on.

Thank Him.

Praise Him.

Love the pit!

If you die with Christ you will rise with Him!

And as Moses lifted up the serpent in the wilderness, even so must the Son of man be lifted up: that whosoever believeth in him should not perish, but have eternal life.

For God so loved the world, that he gave his only begotten Son, that whosoever believeth in him should not perish, but have everlasting life.

For God sent not his Son into the world to condemn the world; but that the world through him might be saved (John 3:14-17).

CHAPTER EIGHT

No Snakes Live in the Palace!

From the foundation of the world, when God created the heavens and the earth and breathed life into man, there has been only one creature that God cursed ... the serpent.

And the Lord God said unto the woman, What is this that thou hast done? And the woman said, The serpent beguiled me, and I did eat.

And the Lord God said unto the serpent, Because thou

hast done this, thou art cursed above all cattle, and above every beast of the field; upon thy belly shalt thou go, and dust shalt thou eat all the days of thy life (Genesis 3:13,14).

Ever since the Garden of Eden the serpent has been more subtle, more cunning, more crafty, more slippery, more evasive, more deceptive than any other creature. With its slimy countenance, slithering mannerisms, forked tongue and fangs bared it releases its poisonous venom into unsuspecting prey. The serpent is a strange creature.

Snakes seldom come out into the open.

They usually hide and wait, slipping and sliding through the darkness, in cracks and crevices beneath rocks and logs. Sometimes they wait for days for an unsuspecting victim. At precisely the right moment, they propel their bodies forward, sinking those venomous fangs into their prey.

Snakes stalk.

Bite.

Immobilize.

Kill their prey.

Snakes Hate the Light

From the very beginning, the devil has assumed the symbolic form of a snake. When Satan was cast out of heaven, he was identified as a snake.

And the great dragon was cast out, that old serpent,

called the Devil, and Satan, which deceiveth the whole world: he was cast out into the earth, and his angels were cast out with him (Revelation 12:9).

The devil lies in the pit poised and ready to release his immobilizing poison on the world.

His aim is to destroy.

But there is a cure for his deadly bite.

We can dwell where he cannot harm us -- through a revelation of the blood, the cross and the redemption of lost humanity. Thus armed, the bite of the serpent becomes no more than a mosquito bite as we trudge the path of life.

How can you protect yourself from snakebite when you've stumbled into a pit full of snakes and no one is rushing to your aid?

Know God and walk in His will for your life!

Then said they unto him, Who art thou? And Jesus saith unto them, Even the same that I said unto you from the beginning (John 8:25).

We have all asked this same question, "Lord, who are you? I thought I knew who you were, but if you are the God I thought you were, you wouldn't let me go through this trouble in my life."

Every Christian has probably prayed something similar at one time or another as they have brooded over their problems. When we are in the middle of a difficult circumstance, it is easy to lose sight of the overall purpose and plan of God.

If we can't see God's purpose for us, it is hard to see Him.

Jesus wants you to see Him in every situation.

He told the scribes and Pharisees who He was. What Jesus told them then is still true for us today. He was also telling us who He is and what He came to do.

I am the light of the world: he that followeth me shall not walk in darkness, but shall have the light of life (John 8:12).

Jesus is your light, and when you walk with Him, His light shines in you.

Now, let me ask you this: where does the snake live?

He dwells in darkness.

Where do you walk when Jesus walks with you?

You walk in the light!

Even when you are seemingly lost in the blackest pit of trouble, trial and tribulation, there is a light ... because Jesus dwells within you!

Jesus continued,

Though I bear record of myself, yet my record is true: for I know whence I came, and whither I go; but ye cannot tell whence I come, and whither I go (John 8:14).

Even though you are in the pit, acknowledge who you are in Christ, and the serpent cannot harm you. You walk in God's light in the midst of the darkness.

Then said Jesus unto them, When ye have lifted up the Son of man, then shall ye know that I am he, and that I do nothing of myself; but as my Father hath taught me, I speak these things (John 8:28).

These are the same things you need to know today to dwell in the palace, safe from the deadly bite of the serpent.

Jesus wanted them to know about the coming events of His life. He wanted them to understand there was a dark day coming when the Son of God would be lifted up between heaven and earth. They would put Him in a borrowed tomb. The temple would be destroyed, but on the third day He would build it again.

He was saying to these Jews, "You don't know who I am right now, but when you crucify me and I kick the end out of that tomb, you won't have to ask anyone who I am. You'll know who I am and who He is that sent me."

Then, Jesus told them, *And he that sent me is with me: the Father hath not left me alone: for I do always those things that please him. As he spake these words, many believed on him. Then said Jesus to those Jews which believed on him, If ye continue in my word, then are ye my disciples indeed; And ye shall know the truth, and the truth shall make you free (John 8:29-32).*

When you are in the pit, you need to remember that the Father has not left you alone.

Why? Because you do those things that please Him!

You are His disciple and you walk in His truth.

When the Jews heard Jesus, they then asked:

They answered him, We be Abraham's seed, and were never in bondage to any man: how sayest thou, Ye shall be made free? (John 8:33).

It is the same question and the same message for us today, and it is time for us to be made free.

Without the blood-stained banner of Jesus Christ of Nazareth, no one enjoys any real freedom.

Only the Son can make you truly free!

Today, a church in Russia is free.

Today, a blood-bought, remnant church in Marxist Cuba is filled with the Holy Ghost. Their hearts breathe free today.

The Son has made them free, and they are free indeed.

Serpent Bondage

Verily, verily, I say unto you, Whosoever committeth sin is the servant of sin (John 8:34).

America is in the pit, laying with serpents.

America is living a lie, seeing sin through the blinders of bondage.

We think we are a free nation, but we are in more bondage to sin than any other nation on earth. The serpent has bitten us, and we are full of his poisonous venom. We are paralyzed, immobilized and incapable of any real freedom as long as his poison courses through our nation's bloodstream.

We have been bitten by the devil, and we do not even have the sense to realize it!

The majority of Americans cannot name half of the Ten Commandments. Increasing numbers of people believe that lying and stealing are acceptable, if they have a positive result.[1]

Nine out of ten people surveyed in America confess they are Christians, but only four out of those ten call themselves born again.[2]

Americans are dying of snakebite in the pits of their sins!

Americans consume 30 million sleeping pills everyday.[3]

America, the land of the free and the home of the brave, has been snakebitten. Americans proudly declare their freedom, but only the Son of God can make us free!

The Son plus nothing.

The Son minus nothing.

You can only breathe freedom's air from the top of Calvary's mountain.

The National Council on Alcoholism says children in this nation see alcohol consumed on television 75,000 times before they reach the legal drinking age. They see it consumed on television twenty-four times more then coffee and 120 times more than milk.[4]

Ninety percent of homosexuals in San Francisco still confess they are not taking even basic measures to prevent the spread of AIDS.

Thirty-five percent of homosexuals agreed that reducing the number of sexual partners would reduce their risk of AIDS, but each one of those interviewed was sexually active with five different partners the prior month. Eighty percent of the homosexual population of San Francisco and New York City have tested positive for the HIV virus.[5]

America has been snakebitten.

Rock and roll stars strut across stages wearing nothing more than loin cloths. They utter profanities that at one time in our nation would have landed them in jail for obscene language.

We have used our so-called freedom as an occasion for the flesh. Like a cat playing with a ball of yarn, we have entangled ourselves in the indulgences of our self-sufficient lusts and lifestyles. We have created a philosophic god for ourselves and we don't want to hear anything about sin.

You can be free ... even in the pit ... if you will kneel at the base of an old-fashioned, blood-stained cross.

Surviving Snakebites
You can be free from snakebite.

If you have been bitten, you can recover.

And as Moses lifted up the serpent in the wilderness, even so must the Son of man be lifted up:

That whosoever believeth in him should not perish, but have eternal life.

For God so loved the world, that he gave his only begotten Son, that whosoever believeth in him should not perish, but have everlasting life.

For God sent not his Son into the world to condemn the world: but that the world through him might be saved (John 3:14-17).

You can survive snakebite.

Out of Bondage

Numbers 21 records the story of Moses as He led the children of Israel out of Egyptian bondage. When the Israelites began to murmur and complain in the wilderness, God sent serpents among the people. The Israelites were bitten and dying.

But Moses interceded for the children of God saying, "We've sinned. What can we do to be free from this plague?"

In answer to that question, God made provision for their relief.

Make thee a fiery serpent, and set it upon a pole: and it shall come to pass, that every one that is bitten, when he looketh upon it, shall live (Numbers 21:8).

Moses fashioned a bronze representation of a venomous snake like those striking the Israelites. He then raised it up on a high pole, so that it could be seen from the entire camp. Everyone who was stung by the snakes was healed as they looked up to this snake of bronze. Millions were delivered from the curse of snakebite.

Not only were they not bitten anymore, but those who had been bitten were instantly healed!

Today, in America we are snakebitten.

We have felt the sting of the fiery serpent.

Our bodies, our minds, our social lives and our nation are full of the poisonous venom. Secular humanism courses through our veins. The philosophies of men and New Age religion pump to our hearts.

None of these man made cures work.

The only cure for snakebitten souls is Jesus.

America has been inundated with the poisonous venom of religiosity. We have believed the lie of those stripping the Gospel of its power. Because America has believed a lie, the church is still stuck and half-dead in the pit instead of dwelling victoriously in the palace!

The Bible says there are those who ...

Having a form of godliness, but denying the power thereof; from such turn away (2 Timothy 3:5).

Churches don't want to hear about the gifts of the

126

Holy Ghost in the demonstration of signs and wonders.

It is time America faced the truth.

The Jews had to look up to be saved from the snakes in the pit.

Today, America must look up to Jesus to be delivered. America must get back to God!

Fever and Thirst

The venom from the fiery serpents is in our veins, and we are running a critical fever.

America is burning up with the fever of racism.

Your skin may be darker than mine, and I may have to pay to get curl in my hair. But if I'm laying in a hospital about to die, a needle piercing your black skin, running your blood into the veins under my lily white skin, will save me.

We are all the same.

Racism in the body of Christ is from the very pit of hell. In the palace, we stand equal, shouting the praises of the God who has redeemed us from every nation, every creed, every color and every ethnic group!

The blood of Jesus Christ saves and equalizes every one of us!

The fever and passion of lust drives men to hug their babies, kiss their wives goodbye in the morning and walk out of their lives never to be seen again.

The snakes are striking America, and they are fatal unless we receive the cure.

With fever comes an unquenchable thirst.

Fever races through our life blood. Americans are dry and parched, trying to fill the cavernous void in their hearts with paganism and idolatry.

They try to quench their thirst with sex.

They try to fill the void with alcohol.

The only cure is living water.

Jesus met a woman at the well of Samaria. He said, *Whosoever drinketh of this water shall thirst again: but whosoever drinketh of the water that I shall give him shall never thirst; but the water that I shall give him shall be in him a well of water springing up into everlasting life (John 4:13,14).*

You may be spending time in a pit, but you know in whom you believe, and He is your protection against snakebite. Even if you have already been bitten by sin and are burning up with fever, He offers you living water to quench your thirst!

God has given you every tool you need to survive the snakes in the pit!

No Snake Can Stop You

Paul was shipwrecked on his way to Malta. On the shore, he started picking up sticks to build a fire, when a viper attached itself to him.

And when Paul had gathered a bundle of sticks, and laid them on the fire, there came a viper out of the heat, and fastened on his hand (Acts 28:3).

You cannot walk through trials and tribulations and never be bitten. Somewhere, somehow, someway the viper will strike and attach itself to you.

Jesus said, *In the world ye shall have tribulation: but be of good cheer; I have overcome the world (John 16:33).*

Paul did not allow that snake to deter him.

And he shook off the beast into the fire, and felt no harm (Acts 28:5).

Paul was on the way to Rome and no snake was going to keep him from getting there.

If you are walking in the plan and purpose of God, you may have a viper on your leg, you may have one on your hand and one hanging on your earlobe; but do not be worried about it. You are going to come out of the pit and make it to the palace!

No snake can keep you in the pit.

And he said unto them, I beheld Satan as lightning fall from heaven.

Behold, I give unto you power to tread on serpents and scorpions, and over all the power of the enemy: and nothing shall by any means hurt you.

Notwithstanding in this rejoice not, that the spirits are subject unto you; but rather rejoice, because your names are written in heaven (Luke 10:18-20).

You can survive snakebite.

The viper that attached itself to Paul should have caused him to die.

But Paul just walked over to the fire.

You have the fire of the Holy Ghost inside you. You have the light of Jesus inside you!

Jesus was living on the inside of Paul, so the snake could not harm him.

Paul knew that Jesus *gave them power and authority over all devils, and to cure diseases (Luke 9:1).*

Paul knew, *And these signs shall follow them that believe; in my name shall they cast out devils; they shall speak with new tongues. They shall take up serpents; and if they drink any deadly thing, it shall not hurt them; they shall lay hands on the sick, and they shall recover (Mark 16:17,18).*

Fear didn't immobilize Paul. He was on his way to Rome, and fear could not stop him!

Doctors tell you not to panic if a snake bites you. If you are fearful and anxious, your heart beats more rapidly and pumps that poisonous venom throughout your body much faster.

The same is true in the spirit realm.

Stay calm!

Fear not!

Paul did not allow fear to spread in his spirit. He knew the cure was already in him.

Paul knew, *No weapon that is formed against thee shall prosper; and every tongue that shall rise against thee in judgment thou shalt condemn. This is the heritage of the servants of the Lord, and their righteousness is of me, saith the Lord (Isaiah 54:17).*

So Paul shook off the snake.

Cast Off that Snake!

If you can't seem to shake off the snakes in your life, let Jesus shake them off!

If the Son therefore shall make you free, ye shall be free indeed (John 8:36).

You do not have the power to overcome Satan's venom, but Jesus does. The Lord of Glory is anointed to break sin's awful curse!

Notice, Paul did not keep that snake around.

He did not hide his pornographic books in the back of his car while he prayed, "Oh, Lord, rid me of this demon of pornography."

He did not gossip about everything that came along while he cried, "Lord, help me kick this habit of back-biting."

No.

He cast the snake in the fire. He got rid of it.

Paul knew what God promised him.

He that dwelleth in the secret place of the most High shall abide under the shadow of the Almighty.

I will say of the Lord, He is my refuge and my fortress: my God; in him will I trust.

Surely he shall deliver thee from the snare of the fowler, and from the noisome pestilence (Psalm 91:1-3).

There is a secret place in God that protects you from the snake!

As you walk in the knowledge of God, there is a place you can get to where the viper strikes out ... and misses every time. He is just striking at dead air because you are out of harm's way, through the power of Jesus Christ.

When you know who He is, then you do not need to fear the snake.

God has given you power over them!

He has freed you from the snare of the poisonous viper. The venomous poison has been swallowed up in the fire of the Holy Ghost burning and blazing in your life!

Jesus is lifted high on that pole.

If you suffer snakebite while in the pit and are burning up with fever and thirst, then look up to Jesus.

If you are poisoned, then look to Jesus.

For this purpose the Son of God was manifested, that he might destroy the works of the devil (1 John 3:8).

If you are bitten with envy, pride, addiction or lust -

feverishly overcome with sin -- He can destroy the works of the serpent!

There is a cure.

America has been to every snakebite cure peddler known to the human family, and is still burning up with the poison of sin!

Only Jesus can stop the fever.

Keep your eyes on Him when you are in the pit, and no snake can harm you.

You will not perish but have everlasting life.

*And, behold, two of them went the same day to a
village called Emmaus, which was from Jerusalem about
threescore furlongs (Luke 24:13).*

CHAPTER NINE

The Deepest Pit of All!

Two of Jesus' followers are leaving the city of Jerusalem after spending four of the most tortuous days anyone would ever be called upon to walk through. They are headed for their home of Emmaus, a town about eight miles southwest of Jerusalem.

Tired and weary, they are going home.

Their minds ache from the anguish of the past four days and the perception that their lives were built from empty dreams.

How could they ever forget all the mocking, the laughing, the jeering, the persecution and the ridicule of this last horrifying weekend?

"You abandoned the family business to follow this

madman," their families mocked.

Their minds are numb.

They are in an outrageous nightmare. They watched Jesus in Jerusalem and Judea as He manifested mastery over demons, depravity and disease.

At the tomb of Lazarus, He demonstrated mastery over death itself!

They saw Him walk on the water.

They watched Him astound the scribes and the Pharisees and send them scurrying back to their camp.

They watched Him wipe the blindness from Bartimaeus' eyes!

They watched Him stop the woman's issue of blood!

They heard Him speak as no man had ever spoken!

They watched Him, lived with Him and ate with Him!

But now, on their journey home, their hallelujahs and hoorahs have turned to disappointment and horror.

Who Could Forget?

They watched His figure silhouetted on Pilate's parapet. They watched as hundreds of Roman legionnaires beat Him ... and mockingly hailed Him as "King of the Jews."

They watched as great handfuls of His beard were pulled. His face was beaten until, as Isaiah foretold, *As many were astonished at thee; his visage was so marred more than any man, and his form more than the sons of men (Isaiah 52:14).*

His flesh hung round his bones.

Now, these men who had been so close to Jesus are leaving Jerusalem. They are going home because it is over! Their hopes were crushed; their dreams were shattered as they saw Him hang on that cross.

They heard His prophetic cry: *My God, my God, why hast thou forsaken me? why art thou so far from helping me, and from the words of my roaring? (Psalm 22:1).*

They are dazed and confused. They walked with Him, talked with Him and saw His miracles.

Now, they are in the pit, plagued by the memories of His agony and death.

Three Hours of Agony

Can you see Him as He struggles on that cross, with His feet crossed one upon one another?

His legs are bent.

His arms are stretched, but not all the way out ... extended just enough so His full weight must hang upon the nails. Can you hear the wheezing of His breath?

The judgment of Almighty God is raining down like fire and brimstone, invading the flesh of the only begotten Son of God.

He screams in horror, "I thirst!," and they give him

vinegar to drink. He shoves his head back and the thorns pierce His skull, as a crimson trail of blood streams down his cheek.

Flies buzz around that cross.

The stench is unbearable.

Men walk by and mock.

Can you see Him there ... seemingly forsaken?

He said, "Our fathers cried to you, and you heard them! Why is your ear deafened to my cry? They counted on you and you delivered them" (v. 4,5)

David's prophetic words of the Lord's agony on the cross come graphically into perspective as He hangs on the cross.

Many bulls have compassed me: strong bulls of Bashan have beset me round.

They gaped upon me with their mouths, as a ravening and a roaring lion.

I am poured out like water, and all my bones are out of joint: my heart is like wax; it is melted in the midst of my bowels.

My strength is dried up like a potsherd; and my tongue cleaveth to my jaws; and thou hast brought me into the dust of death.

For dogs have compassed me: the assembly of the wicked have enclosed me: they pierced my hands and my feet.

I may tell all my bones: they look and stare upon me.
They part my garments among them, and cast lots
upon my vesture (Psalm 22:12-18).

They watched Him hang His head. They watched Him say, "It is finished." They watched in horror as the sun refused to give its light, the earth convulsed and rain began to fall.

They watched. The sun was eclipsed. There was darkness in Jerusalem. The darkest day in human infamy came to a close. They helped pick up that cross from its place in the earth, and it fell over with a thud, with the body of the Prince of God.

When Jesus therefore had received the vinegar, he said, It is finished: and he bowed his head, and gave up the ghost (John 19:30).

The disciples wrapped His body -- the hands that wiped the blindness from Bartimaeus' eyes, the eyes that saw the woman taken in adultery -- in grave clothes. They wrapped the feet that walked on water. They lay Him in the borrowed tomb of Joseph of Arimathea and watched as Roman centurions rolled a stone in front of that tomb and stood guard.

Back on the Road

It now has been three days since that tragic event. It is over. He who manifested mastery over death itself is now captive to the very elements He once commanded.

Now, these men begin their eight mile journey home. On the road to Emmaus, they are full of questions.

And they talked together of all these things which had happened.

And it came to pass, that, while they communed together and reasoned (what you do when you are afraid and your dreams are crushed), *Jesus himself drew near, and went with them.*

But their eyes were holden that they should not know him (Luke 24:14,16).

Their recognition of Him was withheld. They were blinded and could not see this man as Jesus.

Was He hiding from them?

Of course not.

Was He ashamed that He was out of the grave?

No.

The final foe to be conquered was slain. Victoriously He put one foot on the devil and the other on the crumbling empire of death and raised His hands to the Father saying, "I am Alpha and I am Omega; He that was dead and am alive."

Had He taken on some strange form?

No ... not at all.

They just could not see Him for who He was!

Grief, fear, hopelessness, tragedy and trial blinded

their eyes!

They saw Him die.

No one could change that.

Blinded Today

Today, there are entire churches whose eyes are blinded. They are convinced there is no help and no hope for them.

Their eyes are "holden!"

Jesus said to them,

What manner of communications are these that ye have one to another, as ye walk, and are sad?

And the one of them, whose name was Cleopas, answering said unto him, Art thou only a stranger in Jerusalem, and hast not known the things which are come to pass there in these days? (vv.17,18).

They were saying, "Don't you know, preacher, what I've been through? I lost my baby. My wife left me! I lost my job. The doctor said I have to die and cannot live! Don't you know what's going on? Don't you know what I've been through?"

Then he said unto them, O fools, and slow of heart to believe all that the prophets have spoken (v.25).

We have the same problem today as we walk down our own Emmaus road. We want to believe part of what the prophets spoke but not all they spoke.

Jesus said, "believe all."

Then, He said something very peculiar:

Ought not Christ to have suffered these things, and to enter into his glory? (v.26).

You are not going to have the glory without the suffering!

Scripture says, *He was wounded for our transgressions, he was bruised for our iniquities: the chastisement of our peace was laid upon him; and with his stripes we are healed (Isaiah 53:5).*

You are not going to have the palace without the pit!

Too many Christians are running around with only one eye open. They are half-baked Christians with only half of Jesus!

It is time for us to mature in the realization that our God has a plan and a purpose, and He is in control of our lives!

Can't See Christ

And beginning at Moses and all the prophets, he expounded unto them in all the scriptures and the things concerning himself (Luke 24:27).

Jesus shared about Himself ... yet they did not know Him!

How could they have missed Him?

He still has blackened holes in His hands and His feet

142

where the cruel nails have been.

His body is bruised!

It had been three days since He hung on that cross, and they were so blind they do not even know who He is!

Today, we have the same problem.

We do not truly know Him.

As they walked that eight mile journey, He taught them. He began with Moses and all the prophets, and started telling them about Himself. Though they knew all the Scriptures, they still did not recognize who He was.

He was about to leave when they entreated Him to stay saying, *Abide with us (v.29a).*

"Why?"

Because Jesus spoke words of truth?

No.

But because *it is toward evening, and the day is far spent (v.29b).*

They told Him, "It is too late, man. You don't need to be walking this late. Come on in and stay with us and we'll have dinner."

And it came to pass, as he sat at meat with them, he took bread, and blessed it, and brake it and gave to them.

And their eyes were opened, and they knew him; and he vanished out of their sight.

And they said one to another, Did not our heart burn within us, while he talked with us by the way, and while he opened to us the scriptures?

And they rose up the same hour, and returned to Jerusalem, and found the eleven gathered together, and them that were with them,

Saying, The Lord is risen indeed, and hath appeared to Simon.

And they told what things were done in the way, and how he was known of them in the breaking of bread (vv.30-35).

When the bread was broken, their eyes were opened ... and they knew Him.

It's the divine process of the Father.

Like Moses.

Like David.

Like Joseph.

He was taken before the foundation of the world.

He was blessed with the miraculous.

He was broken on the cross.

And He was given as the Savior to a lost and dying world.

But I would ye should understand, brethren, that the things which happened unto me have fallen out rather unto the furtherance of the gospel;

So that my bonds in Christ are manifest in all the palace, and in all other places (Philippians 1:12,13).

CHAPTER TEN

It is Finished

I offer you no hope for fleeing the pit and no hope for living in the palace unless Jesus Christ did what He said He would do.

In a lonely garden tomb the man who once walked about Jerusalem, Judea and Samaria and manifested a mastery over death, demons, depravity and disease was dead. In a borrowed tomb behind the sealed stone door was the corpse of the miracle worker.

As long as He stayed there even His apostles could see no future hope. When they walked that lonely road back to Emmaus, they were operating in false knowledge -- they did not know the last miracle that would prove He was who He said He was ... had already taken place.

How many of us today are operating in that same false knowledge? The apostles only wallowed in their despair for a few days; but today, thousands go through their entire lives without the knowledge of Jesus.

They do not know of His resurrection, so they have no future. They have no hope.

This man who raised Lazarus from the dead, walked on water and fed the multitudes with only a few loaves and fishes was gone!

His healing hands were cold and stiff!

His voice was silenced.

The message was dead.

But the Father of the vision gave a thundering "AMEN" to the message preached on the cross and raised His Son from the dead!

God sent this same Jesus back to those depressed, lonely, hopeless apostles in the middle of their problems and perils. Jesus broke bread with them and, in the process, broke the hold of Satan on their eyes and on their spirits!

Because He lives, their hope lives!

Because He lives, there's a way out of the pit ... there's a path to the palace!

No one is granted a "heavenly exemption" from pain.

When Jesus preached the message of the vision and God answered by raising Jesus from the dead, He gave validity to the fact that His Word is true!

Up from the grave He arose with a mighty triumph over His foes!

It is finished!

The serpent is bruised by His heel.

Because He lives, you and I are destined for the palace and the throne!

Right now, your life may feel like a tomb, but God has already predestined your resurrection! He only lets you go into the tomb to bring you out!

When Paul was in chains and the closest he could get to the palace was talking with the palace guards, he wrote:

Now I want you to know, brothers, that what has happened to me has really served to advance the gospel.

As a result, it has become clear throughout the whole palace guard and to everyone else that I am in chains for Christ.

Because of my chains, most of the brothers in the Lord have been encouraged to speak the word of God more courageously and fearlessly (Philippians 1:12-14, NIV).

Fresh Oil

In this endtime hour, ask the Holy Spirit to give you an insatiable appetite for the things of God.

Ask Him for a hunger for the Word.

Christians who have an insatiable appetite for the

things of God will find that the fire of their countenance will consume the gates of hell.

When Samuel brought forth his oil to anoint Saul as king of Israel, he brought it forth in a vial. Samuel poured the oil over Saul's head and anointed him king.

But when Samuel anointed David to be king over Israel, he brought forth the oil in a horn.

The vial for Saul was man-made.

The horn for David was God-made.

I pray you have received fresh, God-made oil to go forth to impact your family, your church, your city, the nation and the world with the Gospel of Jesus Christ.

Eternal Problems, Predestined Solutions

Nothing is a surprise to God.

He knows it all before it happens and He has already made provision!

Before the stars sang their song in the morning and the Milky Way found its place in the heavens, the Father slew His Son. He slew a baby wrapped in swaddling clothes. The Lamb of God was slain before Mary ever became His mother.

He saw you.

He knew what time the watch on your arm would read before there ever was a world!

He knew how many hairs would be on your head.

But the very hairs of your head are all numbered (Matthew 10:30).

Before there was a world to stick a cross in, He sent His Son. He stuck a cross in the middle of a world that did not exist, hung His Son who had not yet been born on it, and gave Him the words "It is finished" before He could speak.

Before there were any ears for those words to fall on, God had a plan for you.

That plan was Calvary.

His plan was to raise His Son from the dead and break Satan's back while he was still singing praises in the pavilions of God.

We are serving the God of more than enough who provides the answers before there is a need.

We are serving a God who made green grass for cows to eat before there was a cow. We are serving a God who made cows for man to eat before there was a man, and who provided a sacrifice before there was ever a sin.

We are serving a God who created a palace for you before you even knew you would be in the pit.

Jesus was slain from the foundation of the world!

That it might be fulfilled which was spoken by the prophet, saying, I will open my mouth in parables; I will utter things which have been kept secret from the foundation of the world (Matthew 13:35).

He not only pours out His love upon you today when all your sin is under the blood, He is already preparing the way for tomorrow.

When Jesus said, "It is finished," He was saying, "Look, I have gone as far as I can go. I have done my best. This is all I can do. I have given you the way out of the pit so you can live in the palace."

Jesus had a Father and the Father had a plan.

The Father said to His Son, "Fear not, I will not leave your soul in hell. I will raise you up. I will get you back where you were ... but first you will go through the pit. You are going to have to walk through the problems, but do not fear. Fear not, my Child, fear not. Fear not when your breath on the cross is almost gone; I have a plan. You will soon be sitting with me on your heavenly throne."

Today, Jesus is out of the grave because the Father had a plan. If God had not amened the message of His Son, "It is finished," by bringing Him out of the empty tomb, there would have been no hope for mankind today.

Because the tomb is empty, your need is supplied!

Fear not!

Whatever you need, He has already provided your answer.

This is the power of the Gospel.

We have seen the vision of God, the Father, birthed from the beginning ... and it extends beyond the pit into eternity.

We saw the plan in the past and know what is going to happen in the future.

We cannot be stopped because it is God's plan and purpose and His vision cannot be stopped.

He will not tarry!

He will come!

Until He does, His plan for your life is clear:

Go ye therefore, and teach all nations, baptizing them in the name of the Father, and of the Son, and of the Holy Ghost: teaching them to observe all things whatsoever I have commanded you: and, lo, I am with you alway, even unto the end of the world. Amen (Matthew 28:19,20).

He is with you always ... whether you are in the pit, on the path or in the palace!

If you are part of the foreknowledge of the vision, you have a part to play in that vision.

God knows the future.

As you walk in the vision, even if you are in the pit right now, even if you cannot see the next step, God has revealed the end result. As long as you are walking toward the prize of the high calling of God, revealed through the Word of God, you need not fear.

God has already declared that you will make it to the palace!

My Prayer for You

As you continue to seek God in this endtime hour, I want to unite with you in the spirit. I pray that God will give you the grace to flow in His vision in your local church, reaching lost souls for His glory!

"Lord, we bless you. We thank you for your Word. We thank you for your covenants. We thank you that your people hate evil and love righteousness, that they are people of vision and purpose, desire and destiny. Lord, burn this Word in our hearts. Let us learn every day to be less flesh dominated, less mind dominated and to hear, walk, see and move in the Spirit.

Lord, let us declare, 'My spirit is stronger than my flesh. My flesh is weak, but my spirit is strong! I am strong in the Spirit!' Help us get in touch with something beyond our senses ... beyond our minds and our bodies. May we experience the supernatural!

Lord, let us flow in your vision ... whether we are in trials and tribulations or enjoying the heritage of your royal palace. Let us be instruments in your hands to reach the lost. Amen."

FOOTNOTES

CHAPTER EIGHT
No Snakes Live in the Palace

1.   "False Premises: The Assumptions that Hinder Ministry." *Ministry Currents 2*, October - December 1992, 3-4.

2.   Ibid.

3.   Auterburn, Stephen and Jim Burns, *Drug-Proof Your Kids*. Pomona, California: Focus on the Family Publishing, 1989, 11.

4.   Ibid., 24-25.

5.   *American Journal of Public Health,* 1985.